STRATEGIES FOR SUSTAINING
RELIGIOUS COMMITMENT
The Art of the Religious Life

Theodore Weinberger

Studies in Religion and Society
Volume 28

The Edwin Mellen Press
Lewiston/Queenston/Lampeter

Library of Congress Cataloging-in-Publication Data

This work has been registered with the Library of Congress

> This is volume 28 in the continuing series
> Studies in Religion and Society
> Volume 28 ISBN 0-7734-9678-5
> SRS Series ISBN 0-88946-863-X

A CIP catalog record for this book
is available from the British Library.

The Edwin Mellen Press
Box 450
Lewiston, New York
USA 14092

The Edwin Mellen Press
Box 67
Queenston, Ontario
CANADA L0S 1L0

The Edwin Mellen Press, Ltd.
Lampeter, Dyfed, Wales
UNITED KINGDOM SA48 7DY

Printed in the United States of America

For Sarah

וְאַתְּ עָלִית עַל־כֻּלָּנָה

TABLE OF CONTENTS

ACKNOWLEDGEMENTS

I am very happy to acknowledge five of my teachers and colleagues who each read through and commented upon this work while it was still in manuscript form. My work here is most directly an outgrowth of what I have learned from my friend and teacher Don Saliers. His course on the religious emotions and passions taught me to think and speak about religion in a way that bears directly upon the life of the human being in the here and now. David Blumenthal, my doctoral adviser and *rebbe*, indefatigably offered advice and encouragement for my work. Thee Smith's notes were always to the point and insightful. His comments showing resonances between my work and his own in black theology reinforced my belief that in this book I could speak to people of a number of faith traditions. Ellen Umansky has been a close confidante since my first days of graduate work in religion, and her comments on this work are greatly appreciated. Someday I hope to be as good a teacher as she. Ken Frieden read this work carefully. His stylistic comments were especially helpful.

My family has been a major source of inspiration for me. My parents, Leonard and Sylvia Weinberger, provided me with an excellent Jewish and secular education--both formally and informally. My children, Nathan, Rebecca, and Ruth Leah are a joyous part of my existence, and they continue to inform my life and my work with their sheer exuberance and vitality. The person to whom my work is most indebted is my wife, Sarah Jane Ross. Sarah has stood by me at the major crossroads in my life with concern, love, and support. She has also been an intelligent critic of all of my work--professional as well as personal. I dedicate this book to her with respect and admiration.

Atlanta, GA
Sivan 5741
June 1991

TRANSLITERATIONS

The transliteration system of this work is designed to convey to the English reader a sense and flavor of the Hebrew words under discussion. When I quote another source, I use the transliteration of that writer; otherwise, I am guided by the following table:

1. כ and ח = ch
2.   צ ` = ts
3. stressed א = '
4. stressed ע = '
5. words ending in ה end in h
6. all prefixes are set off with a - . Capitalization of root word is consistent with normal usage. For example: הַשַׁבָּת = *ha-Shabbat*.
7. unstressed *sh'va* = ' (as in *Sh'ma*)
8. stressed *sh'va* = e (as in *netilat*)

INTRODUCTION

It has been almost two hundred years since Friedrich Schleiermacher published his *On Religion: Speeches to its Cultured Despisers.* The cultured despisers of religion, however, have not gone away; like Schleiermacher, I feel the need to reply to them. Rudolf Otto, in an introduction to *On Religion*, writes that in the eighteenth century "one did not hate religion, but one somehow held it in contempt like something for which one no longer had any use. One was cultured and full of ideals; one was aesthetic, and one was moral. But one was no longer religious."[1] Otto's words also serve to describe the predicament of many Americans today, including most American Jews--the religious community out of which I write. Religion is viewed as a crutch for people who cannot deal with the real world; religion is perceived to involve belief in irrational doctrines and dogmas; and religion is thought to be a waste of energy: a hobby that calls for sacrifice, induces guilt, and requires great expenditures of time and money.

I write against the cultured despisers of religion, and aim to show how the religious life can be intelligible, deep, persuasive, and worth sustaining. I claim--and show--that there is deep meaning in living a religious life without asserting that one particular way of life is objectively the most meaningful.[2]

---

[1]Rudolf Otto, introduction, *On Religion: Speeches to its Cultured Despisers* by Friedrich Schleiermacher, 1799, trans. John Oman (New York: Harper & Row, 1958) ix.

[2]Richard Bernstein insightfully lays out the rational stalemate of objectivism and relativism in his *Beyond Objectivism and Relativism: Science, Hermeneutics, and Praxis* (Phil.: Univ. of Penn. Press, 1985). He defines objectivism as "the basic conviction that there is or must be some permanent, ahistorical matrix or framework to which we can ultimately appeal in determining the nature of rationality, knowledge, truth, reality, goodness, or rightness" (8). In contrast, relativism claims "that there can be no higher appeal than to a given conceptual scheme, language game, set of social practices, or historical epoch" (11). Thus, "at its most profound level the relativist's message is that there are no such basic constraints except those

As a heuristic approach in considering the art of the religious life, I construct several strategies for sustaining religious commitment. The strategies allow me to address directly the charge of the cultured despisers. They serve to discover how the religious life is still of use to the human being--even if one begins with the premise (as do the cultured despisers) that this is the sole criterion by which religion is to be judged. The strategies for sustaining religious commitment set forth here are thus heuristic devices for speaking about the art of the religious life from within an anthropocentric framework. This work, then, is not primarily concerned with religious commitment, nor with strategies that sustain religious commitment. It is not a work in systematic theology, a philosophic religious argument ordered in logical steps. Rather, it is a work about the art of the religious life and about how certain strategies for sustaining religious commitment are *illustrative* of this art. Because the way I express the art of the religious life is through words, I also pay careful attention to writing: I explore affective and effective ways of *writing about* the art of the religious life.

In considering religious commitment I begin with the premise that strategies for sustaining religious commitment must be strategies that sustain ritual commitment. One is religious primarily in and through the way one lives--and this way of life conditions what one feels and thinks. My hunch is that if I can show why a person might commit to a religious life and what in that life can sustain commitment, I will have done a good deal in depicting the richness of the religious life. This work proposes two interrelated strategies for sustaining religious commitment. Part I argues for the strategy of religion as anthropological necessity, a category that I derive from the work of Mordecai Kaplan as discussed below. Part II argues for the religious

---

that we invent or temporally (and temporarily) accept" (19). Though he articulates the current climate of "objectivism and relativism," Bernstein is not sufficiently clear as to how one moves *beyond* objectivism and relativism. I try to demonstrate one way of doing this in presenting the art of the religious life.

life as artful experience. In order to make the second strategy fully intelligible, however, one must employ forms that are most conducive to artful experience--forms of a non-discursive nature. I therefore include four chapters of rich depiction of the religious life (Chapters 4, 7, 8, and 10). This artful writing in turn serves, in the last part of the work, as a basis for a comparison of depictions of the religious life.

Viewed on another level, Parts I and II are complementary portions of a single argument. **Religion as anthropological necessity**[3] argues that: a) human beings are social animals, and religion is a crucial way that human beings have of strengthening bonds between individuals; b) ritual is a significant form of human expression; and c) ritual is the central means by which human beings in society create, convey, control, and frame experience. Part I also claims that the social bonds strengthened by religion are emotional bonds, and that the experience shaped through religious ritual is emotional experience. Part II justifies and explores these claims; it examines in detail why it is that the religious life acts as a conduit for the emotional life. The two strategies for sustaining religious commitment can thus be construed as one: religion is an anthropological necessity because the human animal is both a social, symbol-using being (argument of Part I), and an emotional being (argument of Part II). The affectional depictions of Chapters 4, 7, 8, and 10 use **religion as anthropological necessity** in this wider sense. In the rest of the book, though there is necessarily some overlap, the two strategies are discussed as separate entities. **Religion as anthropological necessity** (in its narrow sense) is tailored to meet the needs of those who view the human being as primarily a rational animal, and **religion as artful experience** appeals to those who stress the emotional nature

---

[3]I use bold type instead of quotation marks to indicate when I refer to one of my strategies *as* strategy or concept. Also, for stylistic purposes, I occasionally interchange "the religious life" for "religion" in referring to the strategies.

4

of the human.

These two strategies for sustaining religious commitment will be of use to many people of different faith communities. Talk about "the religious life" in this work is designed to encompass many religious traditions. When I delve in detail into "the religious life," however, I must write of traditional Judaism--the religious life best known to me. Because of this, my presentation of the art of the religious life will have particular resonance with those religious traditions (such as Orthodox Judaism) in which religious praxis is tied to a whole way of life--where the various aspects of living can be viewed as movements in a grand symphony.

Though I was raised within the compass of modern Jewish Orthodoxy in America, ideologically I am closer to centrist Conservatism than to any segment of Orthodoxy: I am *shomer mitsvot* (a "keeper of commandments"), but I believe in tradition with change. I always look to deepen the ritual dimension of my life,[4] and in this I take seriously the message of *"na'aseh ve-nishma',"* "we will do and we will listen" (Ex. 24.7). Based on these words, which give the Israelites' response to the reading of the Law, rabbinic Judaism emphasizes that theology is initially found embedded in praxis.

I do not argue in this work that the reader should take up the traditional rituals of Judaism. I am concerned with presenting these rituals as intelligible, deep, rich, and worth sustaining. If the reader finds me persuasive here I will have accomplished my primary goal--that of adequately sketching one picture of the art of the religious life. My own decision to *apply* the two strategies for sustaining religious commitment to the *traditional* Jewish life is due to the fact that, having been reared in the Orthodox Jewish community, I am predisposed to committing myself to the traditional Jewish

---

[4]In deciding to take upon myself further rituals I am influenced positively by the following factors: 1) that the ritual invites family participation; 2) offers the participant access to special foods, sounds, and sights; 3) links the participant with a particular season and/or holiday.

religious life. On the simplest level, therefore, the strategies allow me to justify my own religious predisposition. On a more complex level, however, they allow me to show why the traditional Jewish religious life is *deserving* of such a predisposition. Through my depiction of Shabbat (in Chapters 4, 7, 8, and 10), I give the reader a sense for why it is precisely the traditional celebration of Shabbat that has commanded the devotion of a significant number of Jews over a significant portion of Jewish history. I acknowledge that a Jew with non-Orthodox predispositions could (and should) write a similar study, displaying the art of liberal religious life in a rich, deep, and intelligible way. Jewish women in particular may find my strategies helpful in articulating how they can claim a patriarchal religion as their own. Indeed, I hope that women and men from many different religious traditions will be able to utilize my two strategies in presenting the art of their own religious lives. These, too, would be heuristic readings of other forms of contemporary religious life.

The work of Mordecai Kaplan is extremely helpful for sorting out key issues in this book. Kaplan marks a watershed in modern Jewish thought. He takes the Enlightenment project of rationalizing religion to its logical extreme by eliminating all supernaturalism from Judaism--and hence he dispenses with the chosenness of the Jewish people (only a supernatural God chooses). Kaplan does all this in order to *aid* religion in the modern world: "The real issue," he says, "is not how to render our ritual in keeping with the requirements of modern life, but how to get our people sufficiently interested in religion to want a ritual."[5] What exercises Kaplan most, therefore, is not the fact that there are still Jews who irrationally continue to believe and live in a world of supernatural Judaism, for these Jews are *already* interested in

---

[5]Mordecai M. Kaplan, "A Program for the Reconstruction of Judaism," *The Menorah Journal* 6 (August 4, 1920) 181-193. Rpt. as "The Reconstruction of Judaism," *The Jew in the Modern World*, eds. Paul R. Mendes-Flohr and Jehuda Reinharz (New York: Oxford University Press, 1980) 397.

religion. Kaplan concerns himself most with those Jews who see "Judaism with supernaturalism" as an irrational strategy of religious commitment, Jews who are indifferent to Judaism and who are often found amongst the cultured despisers of religion.

This book engages Kaplan's project: apologetics for the way of life of the Jews. Both Kaplan and I see the Jewish religion as the hallmark of Jewish civilization. My first strategy for sustaining religious commitment, therefore, **religion as anthropological necessity**, was initially suggested by Kaplan's work. Kaplan presents the striking idea that one can do away with supernaturalism and yet still practice one's particular religion because it meets certain needs of one's people--and that all this may be rational. It is a rational strategy because it argues for a ritual system of some kind (since human beings and their civilizations always utilize ritual systems),[6] and suggests that if one defines oneself as a member of a particular religious community it makes sense to perform the rites of that community. This strategy, therefore, helps one to see the religious life as *rationally intelligible*. In my first chapter, I show how Kaplan's work points to **religion as anthropo-logical necessity**. In the second chapter, following Kaplan's lead, I explore some representative thinkers from the field of religious anthropology (Emile Durkheim, Mary Douglas, Ernst Cassirer, Susanne Langer, and Peter Berger) to get a more finely articulated conception of **religion as anthropological necessity**. In Chapter 3, I return to Kaplan and critique his work based upon the field of religious anthropology. It should be noted that this critique will be based upon Kaplan's anthropology rather than his theology. Kaplan's

---

[6]In this connection Kaplan writes: "The fact that until recently civilizations were completely identified with religion implies a very intimate association between the two. The divorce of religion from modern civilization should be viewed as temporary. The next stage will find each civilization once again identified with religion, though it will be a different type of religion from that of the past" (*Judaism as a Civilization* 305). Kaplan's work in reconstructing Judaism may be viewed as an attempt to revivify the association between the Jewish civilization and the Jewish religion.

apologetic project of getting Jews "sufficiently interested in religion to want a ritual" rests not upon his theology but upon his anthropology. Kaplan was always concerned lest a Jew accept his naturalist theological claims (he speaks of God, for example, as being "the sum of the animating, organizing forces and relationships which are forever making a cosmos out of chaos"),[7] and yet feel no obligation toward the religious rituals of the Jewish people. This is why Kaplan develops what I have come to call **religion as anthropological necessity**, and why I do not engage Kaplan's theology directly in this book, but proceed to consider the strength of his anthropology for achieving his apologetic ends.

Moving beyond Kaplan, I turn to Abraham Heschel, who understood that an experience does not have to be primarily rational for it to be worth sustaining. Painting a sunset, listening to a string quartet, viewing a film, are examples of activities that exercise more of one's affections than one's rational capacities. Yet in our society most people (including the cultured despisers of religion) can agree that these are worthwhile activities to pursue. In other words, art points the way for a different conception of value than that which rationality provides. In developing my second strategy for sustaining religious commitment I thus treat the life of the religious person more like a work of art than a courtroom (where each side presents reasoned arguments--with victory going to the most aggressive). In analyzing a work of art, a critic does not offer logical, rational proof or evidence for his or her evaluations; instead, the critic uses the vocabulary of the particular art field (e.g., "brushstrokes" and "shading" in painting; "syncopation" and "recapitulation" in music) to show that his or her perception of the work is an appropriate one. Artistic truth, then, is perceived rather than logically demonstrated. Religious truth may be similarly understood. Religious truth

[7]Mordecai Kaplan, *The Meaning of God in Modern Jewish Religion*, 1937 (New York: Reconstructionist Press, 1962) 76.

manifests itself to the affective life of a human being; it is disclosed through the ordered life of a religious person. Trying to discern religious truth from abstract religious beliefs is like trying to analyze a painting's beauty from a study of its pigments and varnish: in neither case does one approach clear articulation of the truth and beauty that is being lived or expressed.[8]

One needs, then, a strategy for sustaining religious commitment that makes the religious life *affectionally intelligible*. A strategy of this sort would convey a virtual experience of the religious life.[9] The viewer or reader would *feel* what it means to keep the Sabbath, for example, or to keep *kashrut* (the dietary laws), or to pray. This strategy emerged for me out of the work of Heschel. Few theologians are able to reveal the religious affections like Heschel; one senses through his work what it feels like to live a religious life. I call this strategy **the religious life as artful experience**. In the first chapter of Part II (Chapter 5) I argue, using the work of such thinkers as Henri Bergson, Miguel de Unamuno, and Susanne Langer, that the affections are crucial to the religious life, and that the affective life can best be articulated through non-discursive forms. In Chapter 6 I look closely at the work of Heschel. Reading Heschel is a self-involving affective experience. The problem with Heschel's work, though, is that the specifics of the religious life remain undisclosed. The art of the religious life is *suggested* by Heschel but not revealed concretely. I turn in Part III, therefore, to an analysis of three writers who do seek to present the finely detailed art of the religious life.

There is an added factor in making the religious life affectionally intelligible: in doing so one makes it *alluring*. In the realm of the affections persuasion is accomplished through artistry, and hence rhetoric is crucial. To

---

[8]This analogy was inspired by Stephen Toulmin's *The Uses of Argument* (Cambridge: University Press, 1958) 222.

[9]The source for the concept of "virtual experience" is Susanne Langer's *Feeling and Form: A Theory of Art Developed from* Philosophy in a New Key (New York: Charles Scribner's Sons, 1953). Relevant portions of Langer's book are discussed in detail in Chapter 5.

feel that something is true one must first be invited into that affection. In order to make **the religious life as artful experience** *persuasive*, therefore, one must make the religious life affectively alluring--just as one makes **the religious life as anthropological necessity** persuasive by making that life rationally intelligible. To convey the full richness of the religious life a theologian must work on an audience's emotional life--else the account put forward will not be affectionally persuasive. But here there is a tricky problem. While affective writing ought not be equated with proselytizing, effective proselytizing is often supported by an affectional invitation to the religious life.

A writer who wishes to present the religious affections adequately will inevitably be charged with trying to win converts for a particular religious tradition. Yet persuasive description need not be proselytizing. I am not concerned with partisan religious polemics in this work. Non-traditional Jews could write affectively as well as effectively of their own religious lives. I expect them, however, to elucidate the difference it makes in a person's life to be, say, a Reform Jew. My critique of depictions of the Jewish religious life does not rest on the fact that a non-traditional Jewish life is being depicted, but that no life is being forcefully represented. Whether or not a description of a certain ritual has proselytizing potential is not of immediate concern in this work. The criticism that a description is not alluring means that it does not give one a sense for the affectiveness of the particular ritual under discussion. Some may find this work uncritically espousing the major tenets of a patriarchal orthodoxy. This is the risk an apologetic theologian takes. Drawing back from an affectional depiction of the religious life, though, runs an even greater risk: that of failing to present the religious life in all of its richness. A depiction of the art of the religious life will include both discursive and non-discursive forms of argumentation--and should be judged accordingly.

PART I

RELIGION AS
ANTHROPOLOGICAL NECESSITY

CHAPTER 1

MORDECAI KAPLAN
AND "RELIGION AS ANTHROPOLOGICAL NECESSITY"

Nowhere in the work of Mordecai Kaplan will one find the phrase "religion as anthropological necessity." Yet Kaplan was the first Jewish thinker to draw extensively upon the notion of **religion as anthropological necessity**, and I became interested in this concept through him. Whether Kaplan would have agreed with the highlighting of this concept from his writings I cannot tell; but as I develop this concept into an apologetic strategy, its importance in Kaplan's work will become evident.

In *Judaism as a Civilization: Toward a Reconstruction of American Jewish Life*, Mordecai Kaplan argues both that Judaism *is* a civilization, and that Judaism must be *seen* as a civilization if it is to thrive and survive in modernity. Kaplan's argument for the first point is familiar enough: Judaism is indeed a *religious* civilization, but religion--however important a component--is just one aspect of that civilization; thus *"paradoxical as it may sound, the spiritual regeneration of the Jewish people demands that religion cease to be its sole preoccupation"* (345).[1] To this end Kaplan urges the reconstruction, not just of the Jewish religion, but of the whole Jewish civilization--including Jewish art, music, language, and literature.

Kaplan's second point, however, most concerns me. He uses the

---

[1]Unless otherwise noted, emphasis in quotations throughout this book will be consistent with the quoted text. Kaplan's works will henceforth be cited as follows: *Judaism as a Civilization: Toward a Reconstruction of American Jewish Life*, 1934 (Phil.: Jewish Publication Society, 1981) as JAC; *The Meaning of God in Modern Jewish Religion*, 1937 (New York: Reconstructionist Press, 1962) as MOG; *Judaism Without Supernaturalism: The only alternative to Orthodoxy and Secularism*, 1958 (New York: Reconstructionist Press, 1967) as JWS.

concept of "Judaism as a Civilization" in a distinctly apologetic manner as a motto, a rationale for Jewish life: "The conception of Judaism as a civilization furnishes a plausible rationale for what are usually termed 'Jewish ceremonies'" (JAC 437). In other words, Kaplan maintains that "Judaism as a civilization" can be used to sustain ritual commitment. The basic rationale that "Judaism as a civilization" provides is one for sustaining Jewish identity: "With this approach, the question of 'why be a Jew?' loses its relevance. If Jewish life is a unique way of experience, it needs no further justification" (182).[2] Civilizations do not need to be justified--they are either vital and perpetuate themselves, or they atrophy and die out. Because Judaism is a living civilization one does not need justifications for being Jewish, one simply is a Jew--one is born into the Jewish civilization. Yet Kaplan notes that "as soon as a people loses its distinctive customs and folkways, its civilization begins to disintegrate" (JAC 438)--thus the importance of a rationale for "Jewish ceremonies." A crucial apologetic interest of Kaplan's, therefore, is to persuade Jews not just that they already are members of the civilization of the Jews, but to persuade them that identification with the Jewish civilization necessitates certain obligations to the ways of the Jews. Later in this work I will claim that by utilizing **religion as anthropological necessity** Kaplan is able to make this connection between "Judaism as a civilization" and ritual obligation.

For my purposes here, two chapters from *Judaism as a Civilization* effectively serve to examine Mordecai Kaplan's apologetic for the ritual life. In the first of these, "The Folk Aspect of the Jewish Religion" (Chapter 24), Kaplan puts forth the following argument: religious folkways are key to group

---

[2]Kaplan calls this approach to Judaism the "intuitional approach"; it is one that seeks to develop a *sense* of Jewishness "in contrast to the traditional approach of Neo-Orthodoxy and the rational approach of Reformist Judaism" (JAC 182). Something is Jewish not because a supernatural God said so, or because it exemplifies universal truths, but because it is true to the life of the Jewish civilization.

survival; an individual only achieves full self-realization through belonging to a group; perpetuation of religious folkways, therefore, is absolutely vital both to the group and to the individual. In "Jewish Folkways" (Chapter 29), Kaplan claims that religious folkways are particularly crucial to the Jews, and he proceeds to examine how they can be revised to suit the needs of the modern Jewish civilization. Emerging from these two chapters is a strategy of presenting the ritual life as one of anthropological necessity. Just as civilizations do not need to be justified, a civilization's religious folkways need not be justified--they provide ways for the individual to come to consciousness through group identification. This chapter looks at Kaplan's presentation of this concept of **religion as anthropological necessity**. A later chapter considers Kaplan's *use* of this concept as a strategy for sustaining religious commitment.

"The Folk Aspect of the Jewish Religion"

The first paragraph of "The Folk Aspect of the Jewish Religion" contains Kaplan's essential argument:

> Religion always constituted an integral part of a civilization, insofar as it accentuated the significance and momentousness of the particular social group through which man achieved his personality. To take part in the religious behavior of the group was always obligatory upon each member of a class, tribe or nation. Through such participation the group became an instrument for eliciting the most intense social emotions in the human being, thereby accustoming him to transcend his self-seeking instincts. . . . Thus man entered on the long process of taming himself--a process still in its initial stages. (332)

Kaplan depicts the human being here as "achieving his personality" only through participation in a group: to be fully human means to live within a community of other human beings. In order for a group to function effectively it has to see to it that its members serve group interests rather than their own "self-seeking instincts." Religion effectively (and affectively) has proved to be of supreme importance in achieving these ends. Religious folkways allow the individual to identify with the "group-will"--and this process is ultimately critical for the humanization of the individual.[3] Kaplan points to the crucial importance of the emotions in binding a group together. He recognizes that participation in religious folkways helps to foster the emotional glue in a society. Noteworthy too is Kaplan's claim here that the process of "taming" the individual for group life is "still in its initial stages." Religion's work progresses cumulatively: each subsequent generation more fully realizes itself within the group. And as the human group dynamics begin to change, the religious folkways must keep apace if civilizations are to become progressively more civilized.

Kaplan takes this idea of religion as the tie that binds human beings to each other (rather than to God) from Emile Durkheim. Writing about Australian tribal feasts Durkheim says: "Even the material interests which these great religious ceremonies are designed to satisfy concern the public order and are therefore social. . . . So it is society that is in the foreground of every consciousness; it dominates and directs all conduct; that is equivalent to saying that it is more living and active, and consequently more real, than in profane times" (qtd. in JAC 333). Kaplan uses Durkheim to identify the sociological value of religious folkways. Thus, even though today human beings can no longer believe that they are serving the needs of gods through their religious rites, the folkways retain their importance in teaching the individual "to consider his personal existence less valuable than the existence of the group" (JAC 334). The existence of the group is so important to Kaplan because of "the inescapable law of human nature that only through interaction with his group can the individual achieve personality and self-

---

[3]Kaplan does not consider here the claims made by those who consider religion to be retrogressive. Freud, for example, categorizes religious folkways as repressive measures that act to the detriment of the individual. See Sigmund Freud, "Obsessive Acts and Religious Practices," *Character and Culture*, 1907, trans. R. C. McWatters (New York: Macmillan, 1963) 17-26.

fulfillment or salvation. . . . *This implies that one's people will always constitute one's chief source of salvation, and therefore one's chief medium of religion"* (335). Here is a clear statement for **religion as anthropological necessity.** Kaplan speaks about *laws of human nature.* (Later Kaplan will say that "the manner in which religion has functioned hitherto has been neither fortuitous nor imposed from without, but in response to the laws of human behavior," 336.) These laws say in part that human beings, by their very nature as social beings, ineluctably gravitate toward group life because only through group life can the individual achieve his or her full potential (what traditional religious terminology calls "salvation").[4] Some kind of religious life, therefore, is an anthropological necessity for the human being. In order to thrive a human being needs to belong--to a people, to a country, to an economic community.[5]

Kaplan admits that in the future "all folk religions will lose their theurgic character" (341), and so the obvious question arises here as to the relative worth of any given folk religious system (of whatever form). More specifically, one could ask Kaplan why a Jew born in America needs to find his or her salvation *both* in American civic loyalty and in the Jewish civilization--why would Americanism not be sufficient?[6] Kaplan answers this challenge by

---

[4]Kaplan does not show how individual "self-seeking instincts" can be overcome by virtue of group life--perhaps group "self-seeking instincts" will prove triumphant? He is not concerned with the problem that what is truly human may not be the most naturally human.

[5]Kaplan is quick to point out here that *"civic loyalty which finds expression in patriotism is fundamentally a continuation of the role played by religion in the past. It is in a large measure the modern form of folk religion"* (JAC 337). Thus, while many people do not define themselves as "religious," group or civic loyalty is rooted in folk religion; in fact, Kaplan even refers to communism as that "which has become the folk religion of Russia" (342). Communism and patriotism build upon the anthropological needs that folk religion traditionally met. So folk religion--in whatever form it may take--will continue: "If we assume that the essential function of religion is to facilitate the fulfillment of the individual, we realize that it is unattainable without the cultural background provided by the group" (341).

[6]Kaplan is a proponent of the "hyphenated Jew." He says that the Jewish people "is willing to share with the civic community the task of meting out salvation to the Jew" (JAC 336). Clearly for Kaplan, the American Jew lives in both the American and the Jewish civilizations.

arguing that severing the linkage between one's parents and one's folk cuts off one's access to ever "finding oneself" because, paradoxically, one's self can only be found in relation:

> *To accept folk religion will be to realize the truth that the basis of individuality and character is supplied not by the world at large with its multitudinous culture, but by the section of mankind which constitutes one's particular folk.* The first encounter of the individual with the community takes place in the narrow environment of the home, which exercises its influence for good by transmitting to the child not universal concepts and loyalties but a specific tradition or social heritage. Even if the individual is to be trained for world-citizenship, he must begin as a member of the particular tribe, people or nation into which he is born. (JAC 342)

People are born into families that are *already* rooted in specific communities. Just as a person does not choose his or her mother or father, a person does not choose which civilization to be born into: one *is* an American Jew (for example) just as one is the child of mother and father. Because of that ontology, certain demands necessarily follow; in this case, one will try to be both a good member of the American and the Jewish civilizations. Kaplan adds that "a civilization, in addition to other outlets, must find expression in folk religion" because "*it is through the folk religion that a civilization reaches the point of self-consciousness essential to its perpetuation*" (342). To be a human being means belonging to a family and to a civilization; belonging to a civilization means participating in its religious (and cultural) folkways.

Turning now to the Jewish civilization in particular, Kaplan concludes: "If the Jewish civilization is to evoke individual potentialities, and to enrich the world of values, it must have folk religion." Kaplan outlines a three-pronged plan of action:

> It is necessary, therefore, first, to reinterpret the traditional beliefs and reconstruct the practices which formerly emphasized the religious aspects of Jewish life, so that instead of being part of a theurgic scheme of salvation they may constitute a modern folk religion, exacting, while not monopolizing, the loyalty of the individual Jew. Secondly, it is essential to lay down plans and formu-

late criteria for the future course and enrichment of the Jewish folk religion. Thirdly, it is important to stimulate an interest in personal religion analogous to that displayed by other nations in music or the plastic arts. (343)

I am particularly interested here in the first and third plan, as they both involve methods of persuasion. Kaplan wants (1) to interest the modern Jew in a reconstructed Judaism, and he wants (3) the individual Jew to develop a proficient intuitional sense (this is what Kaplan means by "personal religion") in order to judge for himself or herself just what is "Jewish."[7] Kaplan has argued in this chapter that the human being needs religious folkways to achieve self-fulfillment, but he is well aware of the fact that unless the religious folkways are appropriately vital and speak to the life of the individual, they will not be able to "transcend his self-seeking instincts."[8] The "Reconstruction of American Jewish Life," therefore, is urgent for both the Jewish civilization and for the Jewish individual. Kaplan links the survival of the Jewish civilization with the perpetuation of its folkways, and he asserts that the full self-realization of the Jew can only come about through his or her participation in the Jewish civilization. Kaplan says that he wants to recapture what in the past was afforded by the recital of the Sh'ma Yisrael (Deut. 6.4): "an occasion for experiencing the thrill of being a Jew" (182). But just how does Kaplan go about "exacting loyalty" and "stimulating interest" in religious folkways and in a Jewish intuitional sense? What in Judaism will allow for "experiencing the thrill of being a Jew"? To find out,

---

[7]Kaplan writes that "Religion is personal when it emphasizes the authority of one's own personality in contrast with, and sometimes in opposition to, the authority of one's group" (JAC 337). One should always remember, however, that for Kaplan a Jew's individuality is itself a function of Jewish group life: "To accept folk religion will be to realize the truth that the basis of individuality and character is supplied not by the world at large with its multitudinous culture, but by the section of mankind which constitutes one's particular folk" (JAC 342).

[8]Traditional Jewish or Christian thinkers would speak here of divine transcendence, of rising above "self-seeking instincts" through access to the divine. Kaplan is reluctant to speak this language. He is interested more in what will preserve human civilization--not what will preserve human civilization in its better forms.

we turn to Kaplan's brief attempt to do so in "Jewish Folkways," and then to his sustained effort in The Meaning of God in Modern Jewish Religion.

"Jewish Folkways"

The first part of "Jewish Folkways" (*Judaism as a Civilization*, Chapter 29) breaks no new ground. Like the "Folk Aspect" chapter (24), it calls for the development of Jewish folkways to suit the current needs of the Jewish people. The argument as to why folkways are needed is similar to the one propounded earlier: folkways are part of a civilization, so if one is a member of that civilization one partakes of its folkways. In the remainder of the chapter Kaplan suggests how Jewish religious and cultural folkways can be reconstructed.

Kaplan begins his discussion here with kashrut, whose basic idea he says is a good one: "The dietary practices have transformed the process of eating from a purely animal act to one in which spirituality plays a part" (JAC 440). Thus, while Jews can no longer believe that God commands the dietary laws, these "should be maintained as traditional folkways which add a specifically Jewish atmosphere to the home"--not because kosher food is healthier for a person, but because "the dietary folkways are capable of striking a spiritual note in the home atmosphere" (440, 441). Certain ramifications necessarily follow from viewing *kashrut* not as law but as folkway: "*There need not be the feeling of sin in case of occasional remissness, nor the self-complacency which results from scrupulous observance.* Moreover, since the main purpose of these practices is to add Jewish atmosphere to the home, there is no reason for suffering the inconvenience and self-deprivation which results from a rigid adherence outside the home" (441). Kaplan points out that his way of viewing *kashrut* allows the Jew to interact more freely with the world around him or her--travel, business, and social activities are freed from dietary constraints.

Kaplan further states that to give "the home the atmosphere necessary to evoke the spiritual potencies of Judaism," *kashrut* needs "to be supplemented by practices of a more articulate character. Hence the need for various utterances which make the partaking of food an occasion for cosmic orientation" (442). The traditional blessings (*b'rachot*) provide the Jew with an opportunity for reflection upon the food about to be eaten and upon worldly sustenance. A reconstruction of the traditional blessings and grace said before and after meals can show how these "afford the spiritual relaxation which is invaluable as a humanizing influence" (442).

Crucial for Kaplan in the observance of *kashrut* and the benedictions is their ability to provide a home with "Jewish atmosphere." Kaplan is not explicit on exactly how these rituals work to provide this atmosphere, but one can deduce from his work in the previous part of the book that *kashrut*, being the way the civilization of the Jews has regulated its dietary practices, necessarily brings with it a whole history of Jewish observance and commitment. In abstaining from certain foods in one's home, one aligns oneself with all the homes who keep and have kept kosher--bringing one's kitchen (and thus one's home) within the civilization of the Jews. Kaplan sticks to the framework of **religion as anthropological necessity** by seeing both in *kashrut* and in the benedictions the fulfillment of a human need. In the former, Kaplan notes that it is more natural for the human being to develop dietary laws than not. Human civilization proceeds apace with the advance of social and religious etiquette in the preparation and consumption of food. Concerning the benedictions Kaplan asks: "Does not the very rate at which we are living necessitate just such transcendence of the immediate, even more than the slow gait of life in the past? Are we not repeatedly urged to spend a few moments several times daily to relax?" (442). The harried way of life in the present world *necessitates* (even more than it did in the past) what the blessings have to offer: a time for relaxation and contemplation.

Besides the religious folkways concerning food, Kaplan cites the

Sabbath and the festivals as a second group of practices that provide the home with a Jewish atmosphere. Kaplan's treatment of the Sabbath, what he calls "the principal institution through which each Jew individually can experience the spiritualizing influence of Jewish civilization" (JAC 443), will serve to demonstrate his methodology in presenting the Jewish holy days. Much as an Orthodox Jewish writer would, Kaplan begins his discussion of the Sabbath by examining what constitutes work ("*mela'chah*" in Jewish legal discourse). Kaplan, however, says that "we cannot receive any guidance from the list of works forbidden by traditional Judaism" (443). He hints at what kind of work ought to be eschewed: "a gainful occupation which can be interrupted on the Sabbath without interfering with the normal life of society" (444). Later, he suggests that "Jews should refrain from riding on Sabbath eve and during the forenoon of the Sabbath day. The only exception should be made in case of those who cannot get to the services on Sabbath morning without riding" (447). But ultimately Kaplan finds (with Morris Joseph), that "the matter must be left to the individual conscience, to each person's sense of what is seemly" (qtd. in 444).[9] What Kaplan wishes to discuss, therefore, are not the negative prohibitions, but the positive observances of the Sabbath.

As with *kashrut*, "the Sabbath must make itself felt in the home. Only there can its observance be made attractive enough to impel the Jew to effort and sacrifice in its behalf" (445). Kaplan now very briefly considers the various periods of the Sabbath. The Sabbath eve "should be a time for family reunion" (445). Sabbath morning should be a time for synagogue attendance, and even those who work on the Sabbath should come once every few weeks for at least an hour: "It is essential for the Jew to retain a sense of duty in the matter of frequent attendance at synagogue services" (446). Sabbath afternoon is a time for education and recreation. And the late Sabbath

---

[9]Kaplan quotes from Morris Joseph, *Judaism as Creed and Life* (London: Macmillan and Co., 1903) 208.

afternoon can be used for social occasions at synagogue. Kaplan concludes his discussion of the Sabbath by saying that if they are to observe the Sabbath in its proper spirit, "Jews will have to acquire that power of mental adjustment and spiritual plasticity which is essential in an age of transition like ours" (JAC 447).

What emerges from Kaplan's treatment of the Sabbath is that it is the day for family and group life, a day to call forth those "intense social emotions in the human being" (JAC 332). The Sabbath is a time for Jews to be together with other Jews: to pray together, eat together, learn and play together. Practices that serve to further these ends ought to be encouraged; those that do not need to be discarded. Kaplan seems to be saying: "Let's look at what Jews do on Saturdays, bring them all together and then their activities become *Sabbath* activities." Kaplan is not clear as to how Sabbath services can be made "vital and appealing." The "sense of duty" that he speaks about toward synagogue services seems to be duty more to the group. To be fair to Kaplan, "Jewish Folkways" is in no way designed as a full-scale apologia for religious folkways. He *points* to how the traditional mitsvot (commandments) can become more persuasive to the modern Jew more than he tries to do the persuading. Kaplan lays out a few ground rules: 1) human beings need the social dynamics of a civilization in order to reach their full potential; 2) religious folkways are crucial for the life of a civilization; 3) Judaism is a civilization; and 4) to be a vital member of the Jewish civilization one thus needs to practice Jewish religious folkways--which themselves need to be revitalized and reconstructed.

Yet what are we to make of Kaplan's contention that certain folkways can provide a home with "spiritual atmosphere?" *How* can ritual do this? What does Kaplan really mean when he says that "*folkways are the social practices by which a people externalizes the reality of its collective being?*" To answer these and similar questions that are unresolved here we ought to consider Kaplan's next book, *The Meaning of God in Modern Jewish Religion*, which is entirely devoted to the religious folkways of the Jews. It is highly significant that *The Meaning of God* is Kaplan's next work (published in 1937). This makes sense from our reading of *Judaism as a Civilization*. The first point Kaplan needs to make is that Judaism *is* a civilization; but because Judaism, like all great civilizations, is a religious civilization, it cannot survive without its unique customs and folkways--thus: *The Meaning of God in Modern Jewish Religion*.

The Meaning of God in Modern Jewish Religion

After an introductory chapter, Kaplan begins *The Meaning of God in Modern Jewish Religion* by analyzing the Sabbath. As Kaplan's methodology in examining the Sabbath is similar to the one he uses when addressing the other Jewish holy days, I will closely examine this chapter (the longest in the book) and then generalize briefly on the rest of the work. Kaplan says that the Sabbath symbolizes "the thought that God is the Power that makes for salvation," and he claims that the Sabbath affirms: "that the world is so constituted as to afford man the opportunity for salvation" (MOG 60). In supporting this claim Kaplan will be arguing for what I have called **the religious life as anthropological necessity**. He will maintain that the very nature of the cosmos and of the human being mandates the concept of salvation--which Jews represent by the Sabbath.

As can be discerned from his comment on God as being "the Power that makes for salvation," Kaplan is a naturalist theologian. God is conceived of as a force that operates and can be detected in the natural world through natural processes. In what follows, I accept Kaplan as naturalist theologian and focus upon what I take to be crucial for his apologetics--his anthropological rather than his cosmological claims. In this way I continue to show how and why Kaplan is able to present the religious traditions of the Jewish people as rationally intelligible. I relate Kaplan's cosmological claims to his anthropology, but bracket the ontological significance of those claims.

Kaplan discusses three traditional motifs of the Sabbath: creativity (God rests after "He saw all that He had made, and found it very good," Gen. 1.31); holiness ("Remember the Sabbath day and keep it holy," Exod. 20.8); and covenantship ("It shall be a sign for all time between Me and the people of Israel," Exod. 31.17). Kaplan's approach to the three motifs is to "revaluate" them, to appropriate implications that are valid for modernity, and discard what can no longer be used (whether because it is no longer credible, or because it jars with certain modern moral sensibilities).[10] Thus, while the traditional notion that God created the world can no longer be believed, its implication--that creativity *constitutes the most divine phase of reality*--is still valuable. The "modern equivalent" of celebrating the Sabbath as the creation of the world, therefore, would be "the use of it as a means of accentuating the fact that we must reckon with creation and self-renewal as a continuous process" (MOG 62). Similarly, the "modern equivalent" for God the Creator is "the conception of the creative urge as the element of godhood in regeneration" (62). Kaplan identifies both within the human being and within the cosmos a *yearning for self-renewal*," a creative urge, and holds that religion's task is to put this urge to the *service of human progress*" (63), to give meaning to humankind's creative drive onward in the face of despair and destruction. Judaism does so by sacralizing creativity. The Sabbath is more correctly conceived not as a day of non-creation, but as a day for the appreciation of creation. It is a time for an individual to look back over the week that was and to proclaim in a spirit of *Oneg Shabbat* (Sabbath joy) that

---

[10]Kaplan writes that "*revaluation consists in disengaging from the traditional content those elements in it which answer permanent postulates of human nature, and in integrating them into our own ideology*" (MOG 6). He distinguishes this approach to the Jewish tradition from the normative "transvaluation"--which "consists in ascribing meanings to the traditional content of a religion or social heritage, which could neither have been contemplated nor implied by the authors of that content" (MOG 3).

it was good--indeed, that it was "very good." Kaplan points out that creation is a human need, and that creativity itself is a process of self-creation, of "self-renewal." Religion is a way of sanctifying and channeling human creativity, a way of ensuring that it does the most human good. Regarding the motif of holiness, "the idea that God manifests Himself in holiness" (MOG 81), Kaplan says that "when religion ascribes holiness to God, it is saying in effect that life as a whole, the life of the universe of which our lives are but a part, is the supreme value from which all others are derived" (83). Though modern scholarship, according to Kaplan, convincingly argues that "man created God in his image" (rather than that God created man in His image), this human creation is itself highly significant:

> It is an undeniable fact that there is something in the nature of life which expresses itself in human personality, which evokes ideals, which sends men on the quest of personal and social salvation. By identifying that aspect of reality with God, we are carrying out in modern times the implications of the conception that man is created in God's image. For such an identification implies that *there is something divine in human personality, in that it is the instrument through which the creative life of the world effects the evolution of the human race.* (MOG 89)

Kaplan claims that the search for transcendent meaning is an "undeniable fact" of human existence. All human beings *must* create ideals to live by. In religion these ideals are invoked by the concept of deity. In some religions there are several deities; in Judaism, there is God. For Jews, the Sabbath is a time to reflect upon holiness because God is depicted in the Jewish civilization as sanctifying it: "And God blessed the seventh day and declared it holy, because on it God ceased from all the work of creation that He had done" (Gen. 2.3).[11] The holiness of the Sabbath sanctifies life and deems

---

[11]In this work I try to use inclusive language when referring to God. For traditional biblical and liturgical references, however, the use of male pronouns is unavoidable. In these cases I use male pronouns not because I sanction this exclusivist language, but in order to render an accurate reading of the text at hand.

it meaningful. That yearning for meaning in the human being becomes meaningful in itself (and holy) when seen through the prism of the Sabbath.

Kaplan's appropriation of the third traditional motif of Shabbat, the idea of convenantship, is the most innovative of the three. He admits that "there are many today who question the validity of this ["the quest of salvation"] or any other Jewish commitment" (MOG 90). In the generation before the Enlightenment there was no such problem of commitment. The Jew's lived experience of the first two motifs for salvation made the third obvious. A Jew did not need a *reason* to commit to Judaism:

> When the Jew experienced on the Sabbath a renewed faith in the creative possibilities of life and a heightened sense of its sacredness, he was aware that this enhancement of his personality, this *neshamah yeterah*, or "oversoul," came to him not as an individual but as a Jew. No individual is spiritually self-sufficient. The meanings and values that life has for him are a result of his relationship to the civilization in which he participates. The more that civilization functions as a way of salvation, the more intense will be the individual's sense of identification with it, and the realization of its worth, or its "holiness." For the Jew of old, Judaism, the civilization of the Jewish people, did function as a way of salvation. Hence the feeling which was universal among the Jews before the so-called emancipation, that it was a privilege to be a Jew. (MOG 92)

Here Kaplan comes directly to what (as we have seen) was a major concern for him: to reinterest Jews in religion in particular (partly, to get them to "want a ritual"), and to revitalize Jewish civilization in general. For Kaplan the issue boils down to commitment: the Jewish civilization has at its disposal a vital core which can be appropriated for modernity, but the obvious fact of the matter is that a civilization cannot flourish without committed participants. Kaplan says that traditionally the doctrine of chosenness encouraged commitment: the Jews were different because God "chose them from all the other nations."[12] While rejecting the doctrine of chosenness (which in the

---

[12]Every morning traditional Jewish males recite: "Blessed are You, *ha-Shem*, our God,

first place anthropomorphizes God, and in the second, is morally offensive), Kaplan speaks of "the need of some analogous doctrine to make Jewish life in the present other than a burden to the Jew" (93). He finds the solution in the idea of covenantship.

While he cannot believe in the supernatural revelation which (traditionally) established the permanent covenant between God and the Jewish people, Kaplan explains how the Jew of old could imagine the existence of such a covenant: "The folkways of his people gave him such an orientation to life, such an opportunity for the expression of his personality and its purposive direction, that he felt himself and his people an instrument for the achievement of a destiny mapped out by God Himself" (MOG 95). Thus, *"covenantship becomes the sense of the creative possibilities of Jewish life"* (96). But why should today's Jews draw upon the traditions of Jews of old? Indeed, why should they feel at all committed to enhancing Jewish civiliza- tion? Because this is how the world is set up, says Kaplan. Each people assumes the mantle of its parents and grandparents: "All human progress has been achieved by the fact that each generation begins its career where its predecessors left off, availing itself of the accumulated knowledge and wisdom of past ages" (96). Commitments to one's people "are inherent in the very structure of society and civilization. Mankind is not all of one piece and, in the task of preserving and developing the spiritual heritage of the human race, the various historic groups have to assume responsibility, each one for the maintenance of its own identity as a contributor to the sum of human knowledge and experience" (96). To be a human being means to be born at a particular time to a particular people, and to assume responsibility for furthering that people's civilization--and in doing so one enhances all of

---

King of the universe, Who selected us from all the peoples and gave us His Torah. Blessed are You, *ha-Shem*, Giver of the Torah." See *The Complete ArtScroll Siddur: Week- day/Sabbath/Festival, Nusach* [tradition of] *Ashkenaz*, trans. Nosson Scherman (New York: Mesorah Publications, 1984) 17. Henceforth cited as *Siddur* by page alone.

human civilization. One does not need a *reason* to commit to a civilization; rather, a person finds himself or herself to be a member of a particular civilization. Civilizations are human necessities--not luxuries.

But why join a specific civilization if the ultimate goal is to advance human civilization? Why not just create a single human civilization to which one can contribute directly "to the sum of human knowledge and experience"? Because, says Kaplan, that is not how the world functions: "Nature has already organized them [people] into collective groupings that have evolved specific civilizations with distinctive character. What is essential is that each of these groups feel a responsibility for collaborating with all others to promote the welfare of all, and that each recognize the sacredness of such collective personalities in itself and in the others" (101).[13] Kaplan appeals to what is natural as a way of arguing for a plurality of ethnic civilizations. It is a fact of nature, for Kaplan, that full self-realization takes place for the individual when he or she is situated amidst a particular society and a particular civilization. More than this, if we recall that Kaplan said in *Judaism as a Civilization* that "the so-called laws of nature represent the manner of God's immanent functioning" (316), we can say here that a person can only come to experience ultimacy (what Kaplan calls "that *plus* aspect of reality," JAC 315) within a specific civilization.[14] Trying to create a world community or world civilization is thus both misguided and bound to fail.

The Sabbath represents a sanctification of the Jews' commitment to the Jewish civilization. It is a time to reflect upon all the contributions that

---

[13]Kaplan makes a point of saying that Jews do not claim that *their* civilization is better than other civilizations: "Jewish civilization is the collective effort of the Jewish people to organize their community life so that it may yield the maximum of self-realization. But self-realization implies the recognition of the selfhood of the *alter* as well as of the *ego*, and this is true whether we speak in terms of individual egos or collective egos" (MOG 101).

[14]Kaplan rejects the division of reality into the natural and the supernatural: "*There is only one universe within which both man and God exist*" (JAC 316). By speaking about the "so-called" laws of nature Kaplan thus indicates his dissatisfaction with isolating the natural from the divine.

this civilization has made to the world, and a time to be reinvigorated for future contributions. It also is a time to realize that the very nature of the world and of the human being is so constituted as to argue for this type of commitment. If the three traditional motifs could be adjusted according to the needs of the modern Jewish civilization (outlined by Kaplan), the Jew of today would once again experience not only the *oneg* (joy) of Shabbat but *kedushat Shabbat*--the holiness of Shabbat.

Several points emerge from Kaplan's work in his chapter on the Sabbath. Kaplan's major concern is to show how the tradition essentially meets certain human needs and upholds certain human ideals. One may press him to support the core meanings he abstracts from the tradition, but his bravura performance in "revaluating" the tradition is exhilirating. Kaplan boldly asserts that the mitsvot are folkways and that the Torah and its holy days are *sancta* of the Jewish people, but he argues against the tendency of seeing the mitsvot *merely* as folkways, or the Torah *merely* as national *sancta*. The fact that human beings, left to themselves, inevitably create folkways and create *sancta* implies that to *be* human means to participate in folkways, to revere *sancta*. A religious life, therefore, ought not to be viewed as a hobby indulged in by certain "religious" people, but as a human necessity, an anthropological necessity.

Kaplan does not speak about commitment to the Jewish religion, but to the religious civilization of the Jews. The issue of religious commitment perpetually dogs Kaplan. He implicitly acknowledges that his readers may rationally agree with his arguments, explanations, and suggestions, but not *feel* impelled to take them up--thus imperilling the survival of the Jewish civilization. Here in the *Meaning of God*, Kaplan tries to make a non-issue out of this issue (later, in *Judaism Without Supernaturalism*, he will take a more drastic step)[15] by forcefully suggesting for his readers this logical proposition: "I am a human being. Human beings are born to certain peoples who each have their own civilizations. If I am a Jew, I have been born into the civilization of the Jews, and it is both natural, logical, and pragmatic for me to get acquainted with all aspects of my civilization--its art, its music, and its religious life."

As we have seen from the chapter on the Sabbath, Kaplan's methodology in *The Meaning of God* is two-pronged: he argues in general that (even) modern, clear-thinking individuals need to have recourse to what religions provide; and he brings in the particular holy days of the Jewish people to show how in Judaism sociological and anthropological needs are met and ideals are given life. At the end of the book, however, the question again arises: Why can't a person find meanings for himself or herself; why this emphasis on peoples and their ways of life? To answer this, Kaplan draws once more upon Durkheim, and says that "it is only as a member of society that man comes to know God" (MOG 190). Only through being bound to one another in society--through those "intense social emotions" (JAC 332)-- can the human being detect the Power that makes for what is good in the universe. Kaplan argues that human beings need some degree of faith to give meaning to their lives, and that only through groups of the faithful are the aspects of divine truth ascertained. Self-preservation for Kaplan is ultimately and intimately linked to group preservation.

---

[15]In this later work published in 1958, Kaplan (probably in response to the devastating losses to the Jewish people sustained in the Holocaust and through assimilation) proposes that Jews formally commit themselves to Jewish survival. This would articulate "the rationale of the Jewish People as being *to give religious significance to Jewish belonging*, without commitment to any particular purpose to be served by the Jewish People other than that of enhancing the lives of those who belong to it" (JWS 233). That this indeed was a drastic move for Kaplan is clear from a statement he made in *The Meaning of God*: "*Paradoxical as it may seem, if a nation wishes to survive, it must not make survival itself its supreme objective, but rather aim at the achievement of the highest intellectual, esthetic and social good that alone makes national survival important to its individual members*" (352).

32

Concluding Questions

When it comes to depicting the particular religious life of the Jews Kaplan is reluctant to discuss any ritual in detail. From *The Meaning of God* one cannot get any sense of how Jewish tradition is lived. True, one could claim that Kaplan was only interested in this book in charting the various meanings of "God" in the holy days of Judaism; and so, according to this claim, it would be unfair to demand a full account of how those days are celebrated. My response to this argument is to point out that Kaplan usually engages in apologetics in his writing. In just about every work that he writes, Kaplan speaks of interesting Jews in religion and of the problems entailed in doing so. Consider the penultimate chapter in *The Meaning of God*, where the key question for Kaplan regarding the reconstruction of the holiday of Shavuot (Pentecost) is: "Can Shabuot [*sic*] thrill the modern Jew as it did his forebears, now that the tradition with which its celebration has become associated [the giving of the Torah at Sinai] is no longer viewed by him as a historic event?" (298). It is fair to ask, then, how effective *is* Kaplan in getting people interested in Shavuot. Similarly, Kaplan does not mask his apologetic agenda in writing about the Shabbat and the other Jewish holy days. He writes in a later work: "In religion, the purpose of interpreting a tradition is not merely to enable the tradition to be understood, but to get people to accept and believe in it, and order their lives in accordance with it" (JWS 19). For Kaplan, the reconstruction of Judaism always has an apologetic tone--it is designed to persuade the modern Jew to take up the religious folkways of the Jewish civilization without a return to the super-naturalism of traditional Judaism.

How are we then to judge Kaplan's apologetics? How persuasive is he? Here we need to remember that Kaplan bases his apologetics upon **religion as anthropological necessity**. The success of Kaplan's apologetics, therefore, must be judged upon how well Kaplan fashioned his depiction of the religious life according to the demands of religious anthropology (and not upon the success in numbers or quality of the Reconstructionist movement). The more Kaplan can present the religious folkways of the Jews as stemming from the anthropology of the human being, the more rationally intelligible will be those folkways. We thus turn to the field of religious anthropology, which addresses ritual as significant and meaningful human creation. From a brief survey of several thinkers in this field, we will be able to see that Kaplan could have been in a better position to get Jews to "order their lives" according to the Jewish religious tradition had he incorporated more of the basic principles of religious anthropology into his works. We will see how ritual functions in human society, how it is utilized, how it *is* able to thrill the human being.

CHAPTER 2
THE EVIDENCE FROM RELIGIOUS ANTHROPOLOGY

There are different ways of conceiving religion as an anthropological necessity, and if this is to be a strategy for sustaining religious commitment, it will be helpful to have a fuller picture as to what this constitutes. This chapter surveys the work of Emile Durkheim, Mary Douglas, Ernst Cassirer, Susanne Langer, and Peter Berger--writers who are interested in what broadly speaking can be called "religious anthropology." To some extent these writers all examine how (to use Kaplan's phrase) "the intense social emotions of the human being" are nurtured and expressed through ritual action. My aim is to develop a more nuanced assessment of **religion as anthropological necessity.** In light of what we learn here, we shall undertake (in the next chapter) an appraisal of Mordecai Kaplan's use of this concept in the depiction of Jewish ritual as we move toward a formulation of a strategy for sustaining religious commitment.

Emile Durkheim

As Emile Durkheim was the social scientist to exert the most influence on Kaplan, it is appropriate to begin with Durkheim and his *magnum opus, The Elementary Forms of the Religious Life.* Like Kaplan, Durkheim cannot find religion's source to lie in supernaturalism (though for Durkehim this is more because "super-experimental reality" is not amenable to observation than that it is irrational).[1] But Durkheim does posit something transcendent as extending above the individual--and this is society: "From the moment

---

[1]Emile Durkheim, *The Elementary Forms of the Religious Life*, trans. Joseph Ward Swain, 1915 (New York: Free Press, 1965) 495. Henceforth cited by page alone.

when it is recognized that above the individual there is society, and that this is not a nominal being created by reason, but a system of active forces, a new manner of explaining men becomes possible" (495). "Men" are to be explained in terms of the society in which they inhabit and participate; similarly, all products of human creation go toward the service of society. Society is crucial for human beings because "that which makes a man is the totality of the intellectual property which constitutes civilization, and civilization is the work of society" (465). Human beings need to construct society in order to *be* human. Humanness is found in the relation of human beings to each other. This fact, says Durkheim, "explain[s] the preponderating role of the cult in all religions, whichever they may be. This is because society cannot make its influence felt unless it is in action, and it is not in action unless the individuals who compose it are assembled together and act in common" (465). The religious life helps to actualize the bonds of society. Society influences its members when it can get them to act together. Action and that which action symbolizes is the connecting link between a society and its religious life. Durkheim can thus conclude that "nearly all the great social institutions have been born in religion . . . because the idea of society is the soul of religion" (466).

Durkheim claims that when one views religion and its accompanying rites under a sociological rubric, one escapes the mistaken reductionist tendency of seeing ritual as the manipulation of the supernatural. He says that in religious rites "there is no question of exercising a physical constraint upon blind and, incidentally, imaginary forces, but rather of reaching individual consciousnesses of giving them a direction and of disciplining them" (467). The particular direction a rite gives to a person's consciousness will be a function of his or her society's needs. In times of war, for example, certain rites might be performed to focus a people upon the need of sacrificing for the community. Durkheim in fact maintains that rites which persist in the lives of a people over many generations can be *presumed* to be "true." If society is the source of religious rites, a particular rite will be eventually abandoned once it no longer serves society; so "we take it as an axiom that religious beliefs, howsoever strange their appearance may be at times, contain a truth which must be discovered" (486). Durkheim pictures religion as an anthropological necessity because society is an anthropological necessity--and "religion has given birth to all that is essential in society" (466). Religious rituals are the way a society *becomes* a society.[2] When people are focused on the performance of a system of specific actions they become known to themselves and to others as the People that lives according to this Way.

Mary Douglas

Mary Douglas builds upon Durkheim's work; like him, she finds the primary importance of ritual to lie in the social nature of human beings:

> As a social animal, man is a ritual animal. If ritual is suppressed in one form it crops up in others, more strongly the more intense the social interaction. Without the letters of condolence, telegrams of congratulations and even occasional postcards, the friendship of a separated friend is not a social reality. It has no existence without the rites of friendship. Social rituals create a reality which would be nothing without them. It is not too much to say that ritual is more to society than words are to thought. For it is very possible to know something and then find words for it. But it is impossible to have social relations without symbolic acts.[3]

Douglas boldly asserts that human beings living in society *must* utilize ritual to interact with other human beings, ritual here being conceived of as "symbolic acts." Her very definition of "man" is that "he" is a "social animal,"

---

[2]Durkheim presupposes a fairly traditional society--one in which religion acts as a kind of moral cement or social catalyst. Mary Douglas extends "Durkheim's idea of ritual as symbolic of social processes" (Douglas 22), and identifies social symbolism in rituals that Durkheim would not have considered religious.

[3]Mary Douglas, *Purity and Danger: An Analysis of the Concepts of Pollution and Taboo* (London: ARK, 1966) 62. Henceforth cited by page alone.

and social animals need tools by which they can convey information to each other. The tools they use most effectively for this are rituals, and the information most often conveyed pertains to the emotions. For how is emotion conveyed from one person to another? There are rituals of speech, touch, and sign. Greeting a colleague who has just returned from a year-long sabbatical with, "How was your year?," one expects, and receives, the following answer: "Fine, thanks!" Now what was conveyed in this exchange? Surely not any useful information as to the complex character of a year's worth of life in a distant university! Rather, here one person expresses care and concern for another--who in turn shows appreciation for that concern. One could say that what is best expressed in this social ritual are emotions. Douglas' example of friendship is illustrative of this. How can telegrams, postcards, and letters make a friendship? Only by *symbolizing* that the person who sent them cares for the person who receives them. The action of sending is key here; the content of the messages is secondary. Douglas analyzes a given society's rituals--whether sacred or profane--in the same way: she sees all ritual as bearing some social symbolism.

Douglas admits that "we should recognise that the possibility of magic intervention is always present in the mind of believers, that it is human and natural to hope for material benefits from the enactment of cosmic symbols." But, she continues, "it is wrong to treat primitive ritual as primarily concerned with producing magical effects" (60). Unlike Durkheim, Douglas is willing to investigate *how* ritual expresses emotions. Here she is prepared to view the hope that ritual provides as human and natural (rather than, say, irrational or obsessive). She concentrates upon the emotional needs that ritual satisfies rather than on the magic that ritual is said to effect (which can be authenticated only in the lives of believers).

Douglas goes on to discuss the way ritual affects individuals (primitive or not); she says that ritual "focusses attention by framing; it enlivens the memory and links the present with the relevant past" (64). Through ritual "events which come in regular sequence acquire a meaning from relation with others in the sequence." (Here Douglas points to the days of the week: the regular observance of Wednesday as the day before Thursday and the one after Tuesday is the only way we have of experiencing "Wednesdayness.") Ritual "creates and controls experience," and it can also "re-formulate past experience" (65, 67). An excellent example of what Douglas is talking about here can be found in the Passover Seder. At the Seder each participant is "obliged to regard himself or herself as though he or she had actually gone out from Egypt."[4] The experience of the exodus put into the *framework* of the Seder links the present Jewish generation not only with the generation that "went out from Egypt," but with all those who have symbolically been redeemed through the Seder over the course of the centuries. The Passover Seder formulates what otherwise might be perceived in purely political-historical terms (one nation liberating itself from its oppressors) into sacred experience: "And God brought us out of Egypt with a mighty hand, with an outstretched arm, with great fearfulness, with signs and with wonders" (Deut. 26.8). Thus it is the ritual of the Passover Seder that creates and controls the Jew's experience of liberation and redemption.[5]

Douglas points out that the major difference between Western culture and that of a primitive people such as the Dinka (whom she studied at length) is that our rituals are fragmented while nearly all of theirs are performed in a single context--that of religious experience. She writes that "the difference between us is not that our behaviour is grounded on science and theirs on symbolism. Our behaviour also carries symbolic meaning. The real difference is that we do not bring forward from one context to the next

---

[4]This is a key line (rendered here in inclusive language) from the Passover *Haggadah*. See *The Haggadah*, trans. Joseph Elias (New York: Mesorah Publications, 1977) 147.

[5]For a depiction of one person's experience of the Seder see my "Reexamining Ritual: The Passover Seder," *Response* 37.4 (Winter 1989): 15-26.

the same set of ever more powerful symbols: our experience is fragmented. Our rituals create a lot of little sub-worlds, unrelated. Their rituals create one single, symbolically consistent universe" (69). Consider, for example, our custom of "spring cleaning." Normally we do not imbue this activity with transcendent meaning, but Douglas helps us see this as a "renewal rite" (69). As nature begins to awaken from hibernal dormancy, we too begin afresh. Dirt that has been allowed to accumulate for months on end now seems to stand in the way of our new beginning and requires removal. The key difference between our spring cleaning and a similar rite of the Dinka is what we each do with this rite. Their "field of symbolic action is one. The unity which they create by their separating and tidying is not just a little home, but a total universe in which all experience is ordered" (69). The Dinka can take the experience of making a clean home and work it into their whole lives: *life* becomes right, ordered, and meaningful. We clean our homes and, while our homes become clean, our lives may still be dirty: past disenchantment with a spouse, grievances against a friend, dissatisfaction at work continue.

More so than Durkheim, Douglas helps us understand the power of ritual in society. She posits the human being's dependence upon ritual as an anthropological fact--she does not confine ritual to "religious" human beings. She finds that in the area of ritual the major difference between the more and the less religious peoples is the fragmentation of the latter's ritual world. Douglas' work implies that rich experience comes from life lived in a symbolically consistent universe. Her emphasis upon the *activity* involved in ritual is also essential in explicating the power and scope of ritual. As we have seen, Douglas, like Durkheim, argues against viewing ritual from the single perspective of instrumental efficacy, for this "is not the only kind of efficacy to be derived from their [the Dinka's] symbolic action. The other kind is achieved in the action itself, in the assertions it makes and the experience which bears its imprinting" (68). This point carries considerable significance for the depiction of ritual, for it mandates that the person writing about ritual be concerned primarily with the effects of the ritual's action--and only secondarily with discourse about the ritual.

Ernst Cassirer

While Douglas devotes much attention to the sociological functions of ritual, Ernst Cassirer and Susanne Langer approach **religion as anthropological necessity** more directly from the perspective of ritual as symbolic action. As Langer built upon the work of Cassirer (expressing this debt by dedicating *Feeling and Form* to his memory), we turn to him first. In *An Essay On Man* Cassirer argues that a definition of the human being as *"animal rationale"* is limited, for it does not touch upon the emotional or imaginative side of human existence. He proposes instead to define the human being as *"animal symbolicum"* because "the principle of symbolism, with its universality, validity, and general applicability, is the magic word, the Open Sesame! giving access to the specifically human world, to the world of human culture."[6] Thinking about the human being as *"animal symbolicum,"* therefore, gets at the uniqueness of the human being in the animal kingdom. Some animals may be said to possess varying degrees of intelligence and emotional or imaginative capacities, but only the human animal transforms its intellectual, emotional, and imaginative experience into symbolic forms. Cassirer notes that "it is symbolic thought which overcomes the natural inertia of man and endows him with a new ability, the ability to reshape his human universe" (62). Because of this, the human being is most human when it exercises this ability of "reshaping." In other words, the characteristic human quality of the human being is most readily detected through its *use* of symbol in the creation of human culture. Thus Cassirer writes: "Man's outstanding characteristic, his distinguishing mark, is not his metaphysical or physical

---

[6]Ernst Cassirer, *An Essay on Man: An Introduction to a Philosophy of Human Culture* (New Haven: Yale Univ. Press, 1944) 26, 35. Henceforth cited by page alone.

nature--but his work, it is the system of human activities, which defines and determines the circle of 'humanity.' Language, myth, religion, art, science, history are the constituents, the various sectors of this circle" (68). Humanness, then, is to be discerned in the *activity* of human beings. This, of course, is not to say that all that human beings do is good. What Cassirer claims is that a "philosophy of man" must begin with fundamental human activities, and only when each is understood can one frame a philosophy of the whole.

At the end of his book Cassirer connects the Aristotelean idea of the human being as social animal to the human being as *animal symbolicum*. He observes that "man cannot find himself, he cannot become aware of his individuality, save through the medium of social life" (223). What makes man unique as social animal is in Cassirer tied to the human being as symbol-using animal. The fact of human beings coming together for specific purposes does not represent a *novum* in the animal kingdom: bees, ants, and apes, for example, each work in their own society to produce works and behavior of complexity and beauty. Yet animals cannot transmit knowledge to subsequent generations because of the "general biological law according to which acquired characters are not capable of hereditary transmission" (224). The human animal, however, "has discovered a new way to stabilize and propagate his works. He cannot live his life without expressing his life. The various modes of this expression constitute a new sphere. They have a life of their own, a sort of eternity by which they survive man's individual and ephemeral existence" (224). According to Cassirer, therefore, what distinguishes the human being as social animal is its ability to communicate with other generations through the manipulation of symbol.

Cassirer implies that the human being *must* utilize symbol because that is the way it expresses itself, the way it lives. A philosophy of the human being, then, while not glossing over the very real differences in the structure of the various human activities, will recognize that "human culture taken as a whole may be described as the process of man's progressive self-liberation. Language, art, religion, science, are various phases in this process. In all of them man discovers and proves a new power--the power to build up a world of his own, an 'ideal' world" (228).[7] The "philosophy of man" that emerges from Cassirer's work is thus a "philosophy of human culture." Cassirer's very definition of "man" is tied to the human being's activities of self-expression. Exactly what is expressed through each activity was discussed in the various chapters of his book.[8] The way human beings have of being human is to express themselves--through symbol--in art, language, history, science, and religion. None of these components, on the basis outlined here, has any claim of superiority, but, on the other hand, one can say that each of them tells us something about what it is to be a human being.

Susanne Langer

Like Cassirer, Langer, in *Philosophy in a New Key*, traces the human-ness of the human brain to the "process of symbolic transformation," the process by which human beings reshape their experience into symbolic forms. Symbolic forms make articulate "*the sheer expression of ideas*," what Langer calls "a typically human form of overt activity."[9] She adds that symbolic transformation "accounts for just those traits in man which he does not hold in common with the other animals--ritual, art, laughter, weeping, speech, superstition, and scientific genius" (47). Speech in particular, says Langer, is the paradigmatic symbolic transformation of experience. She claims, in fact, that "speech is the mark of humanity" (PNK 48). Human beings need to

---

[7]In light of the horrors committed in the twentieth century by supposedly cultured individuals, one can certainly question the notion that the human being is *progressing* through these cultural activities to an "ideal world."

[8]I do not extract from Cassirer's chapter on "Myth and Religion" here because he insists on limiting his remarks to myth and "primitive religion."

[9]Susanne Langer, *Philosophy in a New Key: A Study in the Symbolism of Reason, Rite, and Art* (New York: Mentor, 1948) 47. Henceforth cited as PNK by page alone.

express themselves and they do so most readily in speech.[10]

Ritual is part of the human being's symbolic transformation of experience. Langer takes up Cassirer's idea that human beings, characteristically, need to express themselves, and one of the ways they do so is through ritual. Langer calls ritual "the language of religion" (52), and she writes that

> Ritual is a symbolic transformation of experiences that no other medium can adequately express. Because it springs from a primary human need, it is a spontaneous activity . . . It was never "imposed" on people; they acted thus quite of themselves, exactly as bees swarmed and birds built nests, squirrels hoarded food, and cats washed their faces. No one made up ritual, any more than anyone made up Hebrew or Sanskrit or Latin. The forms of expressive acts--speech and gesture, song and sacrifice--are the symbolic transformations which minds of certain species, at certain stages of their development and communion, naturally produce. (PNK 52)

One of the things that human beings do is create ritual--which springs from their *need* to express themselves. Ritual expresses the humanness of people, just as building nests expresses the "birdness" of birds; the former is what people do, the latter, what birds do. We will return in Part II of this work to *how* ritual can express emotion. The point to notice here is that Langer specifically cites ritual as an example of the "symbolic transformation of experience"--which she has characterized as the hallmark of the human brain.

At the end of *Philosophy in a New Key* Langer emphatically states: "A life that does not incorporate some degree of ritual, of gesture and attitude, has no mental anchorage. It is prosaic to the point of total indifference, purely casual, devoid of that structure of intellect and feeling which we call 'personality'" (244). Ritual structures one's life of intellect and feeling. It would follow, then, that the more one incorporates an entire *system* of ritual into one's life the more one is mentally able to express himself or herself;

---

[10]From Langer's work one could posit that the institution of prayer situates this human need of expression within a religious context.

and, as Langer reminds us, to express oneself is to be human. Like Mary Douglas, Langer points to ritual's ability to shape experience:

> Ritual "expresses feelings" in the logical rather than the physiological sense. It may have what Aristotle called "cathartic" value, but that is not its characteristic; it is primarily an *articulation* of feelings. The ultimate product of such articulation is not a simple emotion, but a complex, permanent *attitude*. This attitude, which is the worshipers' response to the insight given by the sacred symbols, is an emotional pattern, which governs all individual lives. It cannot be recognized through any clearer medium than that of formalized gesture; yet in this cryptic form it *is* recognized, and yields a strong sense of tribal or congregational unity, of rightness and security. A rite regularly performed is the constant reiteration of sentiments toward "first and last things"; it is not a free expression of emotions, but a disciplined rehearsal of "right attitudes." (PNK 134)

Langer emphasizes that what is shaped through ritual is *emotional* experience. She maintains that ritual helps shape the complete person because it is in a unique position of speaking to the emotional life of the human being. There are ritual times when a community articulates and individuals learn the grammar of specific emotions. Ritual both forms and expresses emotion. One thus sees the potential power of *religious* ritual: besides allowing for the expression of emotion, the religious ritual framework articulates ultimate emotional categories. It teaches a person, for instance, not just what it means to be joyful, angry, and sorrowful, but what it means to be truly and ultimately filled with joy, with anger, and with sorrow.

Peter Berger

What Susanne Langer calls "expression," Peter Berger calls "externalization." He writes that "externalization is the ongoing outpouring of human being into the world, both in the physical and the mental activity of men."[11] Berger pointedly notes that "externalization is an anthropological necessity.

---

[11]Peter Berger, *The Sacred Canopy: Elements of a Sociological Theory of Religion* (New York: Doubleday, 1967) 4. Henceforth cited by page alone.

Man, as we know him empirically, cannot be conceived of apart from the continuous outpouring of himself into the world in which he finds himself. Human being cannot be understood as somehow resting within itself, in some closed sphere of interiority, and *then* setting out to express itself in the surrounding world. Human being is externalizing in its essence and from the beginning" (4). Like Cassirer and Langer, then, Berger maintains that to be human is to express one's self in a social context. Berger partially adduces this externalizing need of human beings from human physiology. He notes "the relatively unfinished character of the human organism at birth" when compared with other animals:

> The non-human animal enters the world with highly specialized and firmly directed drives. . . . There is no man-world in the above sense. Man's world is imperfectly programmed by his own constitution. It is an open world. That is, it is a world that must be fashioned by man's own activity. Compared with the other higher mammals, man thus has a double relationship to the world. Like the other mammals, man is *in* a world that antedates his appearance. But unlike the other mammals, this world is not simply given, prefabricated for him. Man must *make* a world for himself. . . . More precisely, he produces himself in a world. . . . Biologically deprived of a man-world, he constructs a human world. This world, of course, is culture. Its fundamental purpose is to provide the firm structures for human life that are lacking biologically. (5-6)

Here Berger goes further in explaining the "need" of human beings to externalize themselves--their biological constitution impels them to construct a human world.

If *homo sapiens* is the animal to externalize its being, its other root anthropological fact is that it is the social animal. Berger reminds us of the connection between these two facts of human life:

> Man's world-building activity is always a collective enterprise. Man's internal appropriation of a world must also take place in a collectivity. . . . Man, biologically denied the ordering mechanisms with which the other animals are endowed, is compelled to impose his own order upon experience. Man's sociality presupposes the

> collective character of this ordering activity. The ordering of experience is endemic to any kind of social interaction. Every social action implies that the several meanings of the actors are integrated into an order of common meaning. . . To live in the social world is to live an ordered and meaningful life. Society is the guardian of order and meaning not only objectively, in its institutional structures, but subjectively as well, in its structuring of individual consciousness. (16, 19, 21)

In order to be human, the human being needs to express itself; in order to fully express itself the human being must do so in society. Self-expression only truly becomes expression when it can be attended to. Berger maintains that it is only by virtue of social interaction that the human being can *conceive* of its experience. He notes that the human being *as* human being orders its experience, and does so in a way that reflects the nature of its society. There is a strong dialectic at work here: the human life becomes meaningful in its ordering of experience, meaning is dictated by what a society finds to be meaningful, and the internalization of meaning is thus conditioned by one's society. Art in a given society, for example, is a function of the social processes of that society, and not a reflection of any objective standard of meaning. Like science, religion, history, and language, art is one way that human beings have pursued meaning and meaningful experience.

As for religion's role in the ordering of experience, Berger writes that "religion implies the farthest reach of man's self-externalization, . . . that human order is projected into the totality of being. Put differently, religion is the audacious attempt to conceive of the entire universe as being humanly significant" (27-28). Rather than fragmented experience, Berger (like Douglas) notes that religion structures one's existence into a unified whole. From his definition of religion ("the establishment, through human activity, of an all-embracing sacred order, that is, of a sacred cosmos that will be capable of maintaining itself in the ever-present face of chaos," 51), it is clear that Berger emphasizes the human activity of religion, the ritual activity. Religion is so fascinating for Berger the sociologist because it endeavors to subsume all experience into a meaningful order. The fact that religion is human creation (which Berger as social scientist assumes) in itself will not affect the meaning found in living a religious life. It is only when a particular religious society, whether from contact with other societies or not, begins to feel that religion as human construction *can* affect religious meaning that certain measures (what Berger would call "plausibility structures," 51) need to be taken to shore up meaning. From a sociological point of view, religion has the potential to be just as meaningful as art, science, or history. In fact, religion has the ability to be *supremely* meaningful, for in religious rites a society can take up into itself art, science, history, and politics, and assert their ultimate significance.

Principles of Religious Anthropology

After reviewing the work of these various thinkers who are all interested in what makes the human animal human, what now can be said of the human being, and what might this imply about the depiction of the human world? The first thing to note about the human animal is its physiological makeup. As Berger points out, the human animal at birth is noticeably unsuited to its environment when compared to the rest of the animal kingdom. In order to enter its world the human being must create: clothing, shelter, utensils. The human being needs to be assured that it can survive its environment. At a very basic level, therefore, we can see that certain *activities* help define the human being. Viewed another way, we can say that the fact that a human world must be created that is sympathetic to the human body indicates that at a very basic level the human being is linked to activity. Here we come to our first principle of religious anthropology: *Humanness lies in participatory action.* What distinguishes the human animal in the animal kingdom are certain activities that must be undertaken to create a sympathetic human world.

The human being extends the activity initiated for the construction of basic devices to safeguard its person, and joins with other human beings in society to create human culture: art, language, religion, science, and history. Three points are central to the development of human culture. The first is the obviously human need of expression--what Langer calls the "expression of ideas," what Berger calls "self-externalization." Langer points to this human affinity for expression when she cites Piaget's study of speech in kindergarteners (PNK 48). These young children were observed to speak in the absence of listeners. To them the act of speaking (self-expression) was itself enjoyable. Secondly, human beings express themselves in the society of other human beings, and society in turn conditions and makes meaningful individual human expression. Finally, expression proceeds through symbol (the most obvious symbolic system here being language). Thus, human beings always express themselves through the symbolic manipulation of forms: of space, time, gesture, and feeling. So we can also say here that the human proclivity for symbolic expression creates human culture.

This brings us to our second principle of religious anthropology: *The human being is* animal socialis symbolicum, an animal that lives in society and makes extensive use of symbols. This second principle presumes the first; that is, the human being is human by virtue of the activities it performs as *socialis symbolicum*. Religion, like all other human creation (such as art, science, and language), is the symbolic transformation of experience. Indeed, the only way to realize that experience *has* been transformed is through symbol. A number of the religious anthropologists have written on how the symbolic transformation of experience is useful. With regard to ritual it has been noted that ritual creates and controls experience, that ritual serves to condition one's emotions in a certain way, that ritual strengthens the social bond between fellow communicants, that ritual helps people work out social and psychological conflicts, and that rituals sharpens one's attention to a task at hand. Human beings over many centuries have found it useful and beneficial to construct religious systems--which are expressed in the lives of its devotees through ritual. This is to say that a characteristic way of being human is to be religious. It is not to claim that to be human is to be religious--though there have been writers to say so.[12] We are content here with asserting religion's place in the pantheon of activities of the human being. So we come to our third principle of religious anthropology: *To be religious is a way of being human.*

We can conclude this survey of sociological and anthropological writers on religion, therefore, by saying that, taken together, they present a convincing argument that an essential way of expressing one's humanness is through the performance of religious ritual. But what now does one *do* with this standpoint? What *I* want to do is formulate an apologetic strategy. The principles outlined here for religious anthropology, however, have not yet been utilized in a strategy that will sustain religious commitment. The authors cited in this chapter are not arguing for religious commitment of any kind. The writers surveyed are *observing* how religion functions in the lives of human beings, and religion's place in human culture. I argued that these writers stress the activities of human beings in creating culture, and so they explicitly or implicitly maintain that the social and anthropological importance of religious systems reside in the specifically religious sphere of action--

---

[12]Berger observes that for Thomas Luckmann "religion becomes not only *the* social phenomenon (as in Durkheim), but indeed *the* anthropological phenomenon *par excellence.* Specifically, religion is equated with symbolic self-transcendence. Thus everything genuinely human is *ipso facto* religious . . ." (Berger 176-177). See Thomas Luckmann, *The Invisible Religion: The Problem of Religion in Modern Society*, 1963 (New York: Macmillan, 1967). And consider that Mircea Eliade, in *The Quest: History and Meaning in Religion* (Chicago: The Univ. of Chicago Press, 1969), says that "on the most archaic levels of culture, *living as a human being* is in itself a *religious act*, for alimentation, sexual life, and work have a sacramental value. In other words, to be--or rather, to become--a man means to be 'religious'" ("Preface" n.p.).

the life of ritual. Some of the writers, most notably Douglas and Langer, point out that human beings are (to use Douglas' phrase) "ritual animals," thus implying that, while human beings may choose a ritual system with which to conform, the matter of performance is not a matter of choice. We can say, then, that from these writers we do have convincing arguments for *ritual* as anthropological necessity. And if we are careful we can even say that they claim *religion* to be an anthropological necessity--provided we take the third principle of religious anthropology to mean that religion is *an* anthropological necessity, one of several spheres meeting certain anthropological needs. But to posit ritual (or specifically religious ritual) as anthropological necessity is not yet to touch upon how this idea may be utilized as a strategy for sustaining religious commitment.

In Chapter 1 I showed how Mordecai Kaplan makes apologetic use of **religion as anthropological necessity** in his presentation of Judaism as a civilization. In this chapter I have shown how **religion as anthropological necessity** is used to describe ritual and religious social behavior. In the following chapter we will return to Kaplan and consider apologetic *strategy*: how can **religion as anthropological necessity** become a concept that can be used as an intelligible and persuasive strategy in sustaining religious commitment?

CHAPTER 3

THE STRATEGY OF "RELIGION AS ANTHROPOLOGICAL NECESSITY"

At the beginning of *Judaism Without Supernaturalism* Mordecai Kaplan writes: "It is high time, therefore, that the problem of supernaturalism in the Jewish tradition should be confronted with that frankness, thoroughness and constructive thinking with which Maimonides faced the problem of anthropomorphism" (ix). If Maimonides allowed Judaism to continue on in a world without anthropomorphism, Kaplan's goal is to allow Judaism to thrive in a world without supernaturalism. Kaplan also indicates that both he and Maimonides essentially confront an *intellectual* challenge: Maimonides writes for "the few Jewish intellectuals of his day [who] did not know what to make of the human traits and human conduct which the Bible ascribed to God" in light of prevailing philosophical thought, and Kaplan writes for the "vast numbers of intelligent Jews who cannot reconcile the belief that the miraculous events recorded in the Bible actually happened with what reason and the present knowledge of cultural evolution testify concerning all such traditions" (JWS ix). Maimonides thus writes his *Guide of the Perplexed* and Kaplan writes his *Judaism as a Civilization*. But how *does* Kaplan rationally mesh "Judaism without supernaturalism" with the traditions of the Jews? How does he reconcile Jewish life to an age without supernaturalism?

Here we come to Kaplan's use of religious anthropology. Kaplan uses **religion as anthropological necessity** to rationally support "Judaism as a civilization." Kaplan's *argument* for "Judaism as a civilization" is as follows: *Because religion satisfies certain basic human needs, the religious component of the Jewish civilization is essential to the survival of that civilization; it is thus* *reasonable for a person born into the civilization of the Jews to practice its religious and cultural folkways.*

Recall that Kaplan said that "if Jewish life is a unique way of experience, it needs no further justification" (JAC 182). This is Kaplan's boldest apologetic move. If Kaplan can get Jews to accept "Judaism as a civilization" then he can proceed to concentrate on Jewish experience itself and reconstruct it. But this first move at least, especially for Kaplan, must rest on rational backing. That is, Kaplan must be prepared to argue *why* Jewish life need not be justified if it is unique experience. Kaplan shows throughout his works, though he does not present the argument systematically, that his claim rests on the findings of religious anthropology. The only way Kaplan can make "Judaism as a civilization" reasonable to the modern Jew is if the concept is rational. What makes the concept rational? It rests on social scientific data that says that human beings do not have a choice about creating culture--they *must* do so. The rational backing to "Judaism as a civilization," then, is provided by **religion as anthropological necessity**--or, to be more precise--by **civilization as cultural necessity** (which includes religious necessity). Human beings need to externalize themselves in order to make a world (though for Kaplan one needs to keep in mind that self-realization always takes place within a particular group consciousness). Remember here Kaplan's calling salvation "self-fulfillment" (MOG 41). This immediately reminds us of Berger's "self-externalization," and of Langer's "self-expression." The human being finds its self in the manipulation of symbols for the construction of culture. Thus we also gain insight into the importance Kaplan places upon the whole of a civilization. Art, history, language, science, and religion all bespeak the need of the human being to create culture--though here Kaplan is prepared to say that for all great civilizations such as Judaism, religion is an essential element.[1]

Kaplan's one big move in showing how "Judaism as a civilization" is reasonable relieves him from the onus of having to rationally justify each religious folkway. When he depicts ritual Kaplan thus talks of "genuine esthetic delight" in eating a sacred meal (JAC 443); he speaks of how a holiday can "thrill" the modern Jew and of the "thrill" of reciting the *Sh'ma* (MOG 298, JAC 182); and he is interested in making synagogue services "vital and appealing" (JAC 446). Once one affirms the reasonableness of religious commitment, one can *assume* that reasonable individuals will make this commitment; and one can then concentrate on how to make the religious folkways more appealing. Indeed, "religious folkways" now take on the character of mitsvot--only now the authority for the mitsvah (which literally means "that which is commanded") stems not from a supernatural God, but from the commanding voice of reason. Once this move is made, going to services can be put into the same rational framework as going to the movies. "Why are you going to the movies?" is a question that never gets asked; instead, the relevant questions are "Which movie are you going to see?," or "How did you like that movie?" Movie-going itself does not have to be justified in the context of our culture. It is towards this kind of thinking that Kaplan wishes to position the individual Jew. Once one is situated within the Jewish civilization, religious folkways do not need to be justified, and the question "Why are you going to synagogue?" becomes replaced with: "Which

---

[1]Kaplan, for example, says in *Judaism as a Civilization*: "The truth is that a religion is a quality inherent in the very substance of a civilization. We can no more separate a religion from a civilization than we can separate whiteness from snow, or redness from blood. If we want to have a religion that is relevant to life, we must of necessity accept the civilization that goes with it" (201). Later in the book he says that "of all civilizations, Judaism can least afford to omit religion. Religion has loomed so large in the entire career of the Jewish people that its elimination would leave Judaism impoverished, especially since its other elements are still in the process of acquiring their own structural reality. If the glory of a civilization consists in the uniqueness of its contribution to human culture, then religion was, and will remain, the glory of the Jewish civilization. Take religion out and Judaism becomes an empty shell" (JAC 305-306).

service are you going to?," or "What did you think of the service?"

Unfortunately, Kaplan's use of religious anthropology did not fully extend to his depiction of ritual. Because of this his entire apologetic strategy ultimately failed. Kaplan, as he himself came to realize,[2] could not get sufficient numbers of Jews "sufficiently interested in religion to want a ritual."[3] Though his rational justification for the commitment to the Jewish civilization is convincing, Kaplan did not realize that **religion as anthropological necessity** does not *obviate* the need for the depiction of ritual, but is conditioned upon it. The religious folkways of the Jewish civilization, therefore, could not be persuasively presented unless the ritual life was depicted in its full richness. In the context of Kaplan's work this would have meant learning from religious anthropology that the way to depict religion as persuasive is to keep as close as possible to the human activity of ritual, for it is there that "the human" is most disclosed. I am not saying that Kaplan-- no matter how he depicted ritual--could have sparked a massive return to some of the traditions of Judaism. I am saying that his work would have been more persuasive if he had extended his learning from the field of religious anthropology (which gave rational backing to his entire enterprise)

---

[2]Remember that in *Judaism Without Supernaturalism* Kaplan proposes a covenant that will serve to unite the Jewish people. He writes that "the main problem is how to get all who wish to remain Jews to accept the past of the Jewish People as their own personal past, regardless of the particular interpretation they give to it" (230). Kaplan envisioned a million or so "Jewish survivalists" who would recovenant themselves to "transmit their Jewish heritage to the coming generations" (JWS 203). One recalls, however, that in *The Meaning of God*, Kaplan had said that "*if a nation wishes to survive, it must not make survival itself its supreme objective*" (352). By the time of *Judaism Without Supernaturalism* (1967) Kaplan thus implicitly admits that, apologetically, *The Meaning of God* (1937) was a failure. He suggests through his "covenant proposal" that he cannot succeed in getting people interested in religion who were not *already* committed to a religious life and to the survival of the Jewish people.

[3]Recall that Kaplan states this as one of his goals as early as 1920 when he writes (in *The Menorah Journal*) that "the real issue is not how to render our ritual in keeping with the requirements of modern life, but how to get our people sufficiently interested in religion to want a ritual"; qtd. in Paul R. Mendes-Flohr, and Jehuda Reinharz, eds., *The Jew in the Modern World: A Documentary History* (New York: Oxford Univ. Press, 1980) 397.

more directly into his depiction of ritual. A rich depiction of Jewish ritual life would have allowed Kaplan to more convincingly proclaim the resourcefulness of the Jewish civilization in articulating, symbolizing, and expressing the human.

Let us just briefly consider what Kaplan could have done in his depiction of the rituals already cited: *kashrut*, *b'rachot* (blessings), and Shabbat. Kaplan dismisses all utilitarian claims for *kashrut* (that kosher food is healthier either for the mind, body, or spirit). But he says that while "Jews are not to exaggerate the importance of the dietary practices, neither should they underestimate the effect those practices can have in making a home Jewish. If the dietary folkways are capable of striking a spiritual note in the home atmosphere, Jews cannot afford to disregard them" (JAC 441). Kaplan, though, makes no attempt at *showing* how *kashrut* can provide a home with a distinctively Jewish atmosphere--he simply states that it *can* do so. Of course, we know why Kaplan regards the dietary laws as important: these are the dietary folkways of the Jewish civilization. To live in that civilization, then, means to incorporate some of these practices into one's life. Where, though, is the appeal of *kashrut* itself? Do the dietary laws only act as a means to situate the individual Jew amidst the Jewish civilization (the end goal)? Kaplan, indeed, seems to think this is the case. According to his presentation of *kashrut*, the Jew can violate all of the dietary laws all of the time outside the Jewish home, and even within the Jewish home "*occasional remissness*" need not result in "*the feeling of sin*" (JAC 441). It seems that the dietary laws have no integrity in themselves--one can violate them as long as one has an eye on the larger picture: providing the home with a Jewish atmosphere.

Had Kaplan borrowed from religious anthropology for a depiction of *kashrut* he would have been able to show why it *does* strike "a spiritual note in the home atmosphere." He would also have realized that the atmosphere provided by *kashrut* is severely undercut if one excludes eating outside the home from its precincts. *Kashrut* is very much a rite that can order one's experience. In telling oneself "this I can eat, this I cannot eat," one is regulating the physical sustenance of one's body. If this regulating proceeds, as it does in *kashrut*, from the well-spring of centuries-old tradition, one becomes rooted in that civilization. Yet this rite is tied to the entire process of eating: from the slaughter of animals, to the preparation of food, to consumption--inside and outside one's home. Ironically, Kaplan mystifies *kashrut* by invoking the concept of "Jewish atmosphere" without explaining *kashrut's* role in providing that atmosphere. *Kashrut* does not magically zap a person's home with "Jewish atmosphere"; it regulates the way persons and families consume food. Consider the following two individuals, a man and a woman: both individuals eat out fifteen meals a week. The woman, though, keeps kosher only when she eats out; the man, only when he eats at home. Now, while it might be true that the man keeps a kosher home, which individual lives a life that is more ordered according to the dietary folkways? The woman, of course; more of her eating is done within the framework of *kashrut*. *What Kaplan argues for are "Jewish homes"--not* kashrut! To be sure, he understands that a Jewish home is made Jewish in part by *kashrut*, but he has no access to making *kashrut* appealing since he radically departs from its basic activity: the ordering of one's dietary life.

Kaplan similarly misses the point about blessings--what he calls "various utterances." He concentrates upon the thought processes that are touched off by the language of the blessing, arguing that "a meal in a Jewish household where everyone washes his hands and recites the benediction, becomes not merely an occasion for satisfying hunger, but a social and spiritual act. The initial benediction can call to mind in a swift flash the cooperative process beginning with the plowing and the sowing to the moment the food is brought on the table" (JAC 442-443). Eating thus becomes more leisurely, as the blessings allow people "to spend a few moments several times daily to relax." Kaplan completely gets away from the actual activity of saying a blessing over food. Blessings are moments of supreme *concentration*--not relaxation. A blessing allows one to concentrate upon the food about to be eaten: it focuses one's attention by framing the experience of eating. Eating becomes an important act in itself, even (as Kaplan suggests) a sacred act. Eating, therefore, is not to be relegated to something one does while reading, watching television, or talking. One can express one's self even through the act of eating; one can make the experience of eating valuable. *Thoughts* about how the food got to one's table are important, but are not of the first order of experience in the blessings.

As with what was said about *kashrut*, I am not suggesting here that Kaplan is wrong in what he says about the blessings--he just does not make them "vital and appealing." In order to do so he would have to show that the activity itself of blessing one's food is important. Blessings are ritual actions-- not thoughts. Considering the thoughts a blessing might arouse will only affect a person who already partakes of the activity of blessing. The way to interest a person in the activity of blessing is by describing as accurately as possible the ritual offering of a blessing.

Immediately striking about Kaplan's depiction of the Sabbath is that the word "*kiddush*" is entirely absent--both in *Judaism as a Civilization* and in *The Meaning of God*.[4] The "*Kiddush*" (said on Friday night and Saturday noon) is the prayer through which a person (literally) "sanctifies" the seventh day by turning it into Shabbat. It is hard to conceive of a Sabbath without some kind of activity of *kiddush*. Shabbat without *kiddush* is Saturday.

---

[4]Kaplan does mention the word "*kiddush*" once in *Judaism as a Civilization* as one example of "ritual forms which help to give Jewish worship its distinctive character" (348). Kaplan does not elaborate further on "*kiddush*."

Kaplan's omission of *kiddush* is even more striking when one considers that Kaplan prefers to concentrate not on the negative prohibitions of the Sabbath, but on the positive affirmations one can make on Shabbat. What Kaplan does say about the prohibition of riding on the Sabbath, however, reveals a type of misunderstanding similar to that which he exhibited with *kashrut*. He urges Jews to abstain from riding from Friday night to Sabbath noon, but does not counsel against riding on the Sabbath after that time. One would want to ask here why the prohibition on riding, if indeed it is a vital one, is not extended for the whole of Shabbat? If Kaplan was making a concession to what could realistically be demanded from people he should have said so (as he later does in his remarks about barring young people from playing sports on Sabbath afternoons, JAC 446-447). As Kaplan leaves it, the prohibition on riding is relegated to another means to the ends of living in a Jewish civilization. But, to repeat, unless Kaplan can make the means vital in themselves, they will not be pursued.

What Kaplan says about the Sabbath and its traditional motifs furthers his goal of "revaluating" the tradition, but cannot have enduring effect in bringing many Jews to take up the tradition. One may agree with the desiderata of the Jewish civilization and with having a "Jewish home," but remain uncommitted to living within that civilization or to making that home. We recall that Kaplan was always as concerned with living a tradition as with interpreting it: "In religion, the purpose of interpreting a tradition is not merely to enable the tradition to be understood, but to get people to accept and believe in it, and order their lives in accordance with it" (JWS 19). Yet Kaplan does not make the religious life alluring. He has some important things to contribute in his interpretation of the Sabbath, but he circles around the life of the Sabbath without ever penetrating into its experience. Any Shabbat experience must make use of a number of the following elements: candle lighting, *Kiddush, motsi* (the blessing over bread), festive meals, prayer (including song), *oneg Shabbat* (the "joy" of Shabbat), and Havdalah (the rite that marks the transition from Sabbath to weekday). These are elements usually associated only with the contemporary Orthodox movement, and derive from the rabbinic civilization of the Jews (extending from the first through the eighteenth centuries of the common era). But the fact of the matter is that in almost two centuries of reform, no major ritual element has come to be added to the experience of Shabbat. Thus, when a Reform or Reconstructionist Jew wants to celebrate the Shabbat he or she will utilize some of the above elements. To be sure, a Reform Jew's experience of the Shabbat will differ from an Orthodox Jew's experience: there may be a guitar player leading an egalitarian late Friday-night service in English, for example, rather than an early service in Hebrew with separate seating for men and women. Also, the category of *"oneg Shabbat"* is very broad and could cover everything from going to a baseball game, to attending a concert, to white-water rafting, to taking an afternoon nap. Yet a person whose Shabbat, say, consists solely of conscientiously going to the symphony every Friday night is divorcing himself or herself from the way the Jewish people has come to celebrate Shabbat. Of course, it could very well be that five hundred years from now going to the symphony will precisely be the way Jews celebrate the Shabbat. Even a person who uncannily foresees this, however, would have to show not only how an interpretation of the Jewish tradition can lead to this practice, but also how a life lived according to this ritual comes to be persuasive and worth sustaining. For the rest of Jewry, Shabbat celebration will include some of the traditional rabbinic elements--since they are what the current civilization of Jews recognizes as celebratory of Shabbat. Similarly, when a Jew comes to celebrate the Passover he or she will need to partici-pate in a Passover Seder. A "Freedom Ride" for civil rights, for instance, cannot be an alternative for the celebration of *Pesach*.

I am making two points here: the first is, following Kaplan, that there is a need for interpreting the tradition in a way that gets "people to accept and believe in it, and order their lives in accordance with it." The second point here is that *there is a tradition.* I speak not of an Orthodox, rabbinic, or Reform tradition, but a tradition in the civilizational sense--the religious folkways of the Jews. We can certainly debate elements of the tradition; but let us not say that a Jew today can celebrate the Sabbath without *Kiddush*, or Passover without a Seder, or Rosh Hashanah without hearing the Shofar (ram's horn), or Succot without sitting in a Succah. To do so would be to say that there are no religious folkways of the Jewish people, that there are no rituals that the people deems holy. We are not talking about "Who Is A Jew?" here, or with designating "good" or "bad" Jews. We are trying to explore how it is that a tradition comes to be intelligible, deep, persuasive, and worth-sustaining. The question is: how does one convey this?

We learned from religious anthropology that what makes a particular ritual experience alluring is the activity of the ritual. It is only through this activity that the spiritual reality of the rite will be disclosed. Commentary and interpretation of the ritual can, at best, bolster the practices of those who are already committed to the particular ritual; at worst, it leads to a reductionist account of the ritual so that the ritual becomes merely its commentary--its meaning said to reside in thoughts rather than action. The danger here is that the ritual can become something to be dispensed with once one gets the appropriate thoughts from somewhere else.[5] Kaplan was well aware of all this. He notes with disapproval that in the first-century Jewish community in Alexandria "it soon became apparent that, if one could contemplate the pure meanings which the religious precepts were intended

---

[5]This is particularly apparent in a secular consumer society, such as the United States, which emphasizes saving time and saving money in order to have more free time and free money to consume more things. If the value of Passover, for example, can be reduced to the value of freedom, then *thinking* about the importance of freedom would be, in terms of saving time and money, preferable to conducting a Passover Seder.

to convey, actual performance would only distract from contemplation" (JAC 434). Yet Kaplan's method of "revaluating" the tradition comes perilously close to what he finds fault with in the Alexandrian Jewish community. By articulating the three traditional motifs of Shabbat, for example, without depicting the ritual activity of Shabbat, Kaplan does not show how the actual performance of the various rituals associated with Shabbat enhances (rather than distracts) from the contemplation of creativity, holiness, and covenant-ship.

Kaplan, in my judgment, underestimated the inherent importance of ritual activity. Even after studying Durkheim, who warned against reduction-ist approaches to ritual, Kaplan could write that "primitive religion is the product of man's mental feebleness. Being too immature to think out the connection between the various elements in nature and the part they play in making life possible and supplying his needs, he jumped to the conclusion that every object had a spirit of its own which was just as fitful and subject to whims as he was" (MOG 196). *For Kaplan, what makes ritual worth practicing for moderns is always the activity* plus *what one can say about the activity.* Without the framework of a concept such as "Judaism as a civilization" Jewish rituals as Kaplan presents them lose all meaning. And while it is true that a framework is necessary in order to identify a ritual as belonging to a particular ritual system (thus rituals are Jewish only when they are put into some kind of Jewish context, and so vegetarians, for example, can be said to keep kosher only when they identify their eating habits as part of a Jewish way of life), yet, as we have seen from religious anthropology, ritual activity itself is meaningful: it is a way of self-externalization and of ordering one's experience. Jewish rituals, therefore, can be meaningful both in that they give expression to fundamental anthropological needs (**religion as anthropological necessity**), and in that they are the particular rituals of one's people--and one follows the folkways of one's people ("Judaism as a civilization"). Kaplan assumed that once Jews were rationally persuaded as to the validity of "Judaism as a civilization" they would be interested enough in religion to want a ritual. But interest in ritual is only stimulated by the ritual. What Kaplan wanted to accomplish with "Judaism as a civilization" could only have been done had Kaplan learned what religious anthropology has to say about the depiction of ritual. He then would have realized that what can sustain religious commitment is *both the rational backing to "Judaism as a civilization" provided by religion as anthropological necessity and the rich depiction of ritual activity--through which religion as anthropological necessity comes to be disclosed.*

To use **religion as anthropological necessity** as a strategy for sustaining religious commitment, therefore, means to be both attentive to one's ritual practices so that one can gain insight into how they shape and control experience, and to realize that the "shaping and controlling of experience" is one way human beings have of being human. The insights of religious anthropology provide a rational way of sustaining religious commitment, but such insights also demand recognition of the power of ritual. The reasonableness of ritual in this strategy is conditioned upon finding how religious rites *are* a manifestation of fundamental attitudes and passions toward the elemental features of existence. Where one goes to find this information will vary. One can go to several different accounts of the ritual life (theological, phenomenological, historical; from one's own, or from another tradition), and then, with renewed insight into the nature of ritual, turn back to one's traditional ritual practices to see how a particular ritual functions and makes for human self-fulfillment within human community. The ritual will be seen to be valuable in itself; more than this, the commitment to ritual practice will be strengthened. Ritual life becomes artful life--one which takes practice and cultivation, one which can express ideas and feelings, one which orders human experience into the wholly/holy human.

CHAPTER 4

DEPICTION: *KABBALAT SHABBAT*

The very phrase "*Kabbalat Shabbat*" ("welcoming the Sabbath") is instructive. The presence of Shabbat in this world is not dependent upon human beings. Unlike the holidays of the Jewish year whose observance is linked to the human proclamation of a new moon, Shabbat comes with or without human bidding. One can welcome the Shabbat with open arms like a lover with a beloved, or one can ignore Shabbat and it becomes home-less; but every Friday night the Shabbat appears. The week is suffused with the presence of Shabbat. This may be thought of in several ways: the first three days of the work week may seem colored by the previous Shabbat, the latter three with anticipation for the coming Shabbat; or the entire week may be seen as a countdown to the Shabbat. Accordingly, the days of the week are referred to on official documents (such as the *ketubah*, the marriage contract) as, for example, "*ba-sh'lishi be-Shabbat Re'eh*": "on the third day of *Shabbat Re'eh*" (the name of the portion read in synagogue on that coming Shabbat). Each of the days of the week exists in reference to the coming Shabbat. Indeed, the fact that the seventh day of the week is not called "*yom shevi'i*" ("the seventh day") though the first six are named according to their position in the week, tells us that Shabbat is not on the same plane of time as the other days of the week. Shabbat is *kodesh* (holy); days one through six are *chol* (profane).

Come Thursday afternoon it is already appropriate to end an exchange with a fellow Jew with "Have a good Shabbes" (particularly if one will not see that person on Shabbat itself).[1] The day before Shabbat is not just *yom shishi*, the sixth day of the week, but *erev Shabbat*--Sabbath eve (and in Jewish tradition, the afternoon preceding a day takes on some of the flavor of that day--thus Thursday afternoon is the period of time before *erev Shabbat* begins). Because Shabbat is always prompt, coming at sundown every Friday evening, there is a sense of urgency that descends upon traditional Jewish households on Fridays.[2] By Friday afternoon the devil is said to be overseeing the Sabbath preparations; that is, Friday afternoons, as the clock ticks down to Shabbat, are the perfect opportunities for the *satan* to ignite a vicious family argument that could have repercussions for one's whole experience of the impending Shabbat. Here we see the wisdom of the sages. In calling Jews' attention to the fact that *satan* is just looking to start trouble right before Shabbat, the tradition addresses a problem and meets it head on. There *are* many things to get done before Shabbat begins: guests need to be invited, food purchased, timers programmed and lights checked so that electricity need not be manually sparked or extinguished on Shabbat; and there is cooking, baking, cleaning, and washing to be done. Now with one hour to go before candle lighting, and a pot of meat roasting, cake rising, dirty dishes in the sink soaking, hot water becoming tepid, and a child screaming somewhere in the house, it is easy to see domestic trouble abrewing. The sages could not make the hustle and bustle disappear, but they could call people's attention to the potential for strife. *Knowing* that *satan* is just itching to ruin one's Shabbat makes a person think twice before

---

[1]The two principle greetings on Shabbat, "Good Shabbes," and "Shabbat Shalom," reflect variant Hebrew pronunciations and ethnic origins--the former being Ashkenazic (European), the latter, Sephardic (Spanish, Portuguese, and Israeli). I will occasionally use the Ashkenazic pronunciation, for though I was educated in the Sephardic tradition, my Jewish communal life is rooted in the Ashkenazic world.

[2]By "traditional" I mean those families who abstain not just from work on Shabbat, but from *mela'chah*--the Jewish legal definition of work that encompasses 39 main activities (*avot mela'chah*) and many subcategories (*toledot*). See Pinchas H. Peli, *Shabbat Shalom: A Renewed Encounter With the Sabbath* (Washington, D.C.: B'nai Brith Books, 1988) 33-36.

barking out a remark that could cause pain to a loved one.

Finally sundown arrives and the woman of the house lights the Shabbat candles. For children, there is something magical about watching their mother usher in the Shabbat. I remember my mother waving her hands before she quietly recited the blessing over the candles. It always seemed as if she was physically welcoming in the Shabbat with her hands--before the roll of the hands, weekday; afterwards: "Good Shabbes" says Mom as she kisses each one of us. This is what the beginning of Shabbat is about: making the transition from *chol* to *kodesh*, from weekday to Sabbath, from secular time to holy time, to when (as Heschel says) "eternity utters a day."

Just as physical action ushers in the Sabbath for the person lighting the candles, for me, the activity of going and returning home from *shul* (synagogue) bridges the span of *chol* to *kodesh*. What is absolutely crucial for me on Friday evenings is to leave my home and return after a while--the actual services at synagogue are of secondary importance. By leaving my house I can physically imitate the time change from *chol* to *kodesh*. I leave my house bathed in the dying rays of a secular week, and come back to a house swathed in the richness of Shabbat. To me, this leaving and coming is *Kabbalat Shabbat*. In effect, I bring Shabbat home (for my wife, this was done through the act of lighting the candles). To so order one's life that every Friday evening one leaves all behind takes some doing;[3] but in controlling one's experience in this way one is making a powerful statement as to the values one chooses to live by--values that the Shabbat promotes.

The synagogue service for Friday evening is itself called "*Kabbalat*

---

[3] I am well aware that in most Jewish households the fact that the woman stays home and the man goes out on Friday nights represents an inequitable arrangement. In my family, however, I do just about all of the cooking and baking, and am home for most of the day. I therefore feel that the tradition need not be observed as inherently sexist. As I hope will become clear, the way my wife Sarah and I practice the traditional life is sensitive to the needs of both the female and the male.

Shabbat" (it is preceded by the short afternoon service for weekdays). For me, the more congregational singing there is in a service, the more vital it is. I especially like to attend *Kabbalat Shabbat* services that begin with an added song called "*Yedid Nefesh*" ("The Soul's Beloved"). By joining in song with the congregation the sense of Shabbat descends. The songs of Shabbat carry with them the flavor of Shabbat. The music penetrates into one's soul, bringing with it the *neshamah yeterah*, the additional Shabbat soul. Significantly, the service opens with "*Lechu neranenah la-Shem*": "Let us sing to God" (Psalm 95). Shabbat begins with song. The Friday night service is a time for rejoicing: one has made it to another Shabbat. Despite all the vicissitudes of the previous week, one has conquered them and can now sing "*lecha dodi likrat kalah p'nei Shabbat nekablah*": "Come my Beloved to greet the bride; let us welcome the Shabbat presence." The little obsessions of the work week that monopolized one's time are now something to be laughed at as we sing "*Mizmor shir le-yom ha-Shabbat*": "A psalm, a song for the Sabbath day" (Psalm 92). All the petty heartaches that energized our bodies over the week are recollected amidst the tranquillity of the One "Who spreads the shelter of peace upon us, upon all of his people Israel, and upon Jerusalem" (*Siddur* 337). My troubles were trivial. How easy was it to put my life in order when compared with what God had to do: "*Va-yechal elokim ba-yom ha-shivi'i me-kol melachto asher 'asah*": "And God completed His work on the seventh day" (Gen. 2.2).

It has become a custom to recite the *Kiddush* prayer in *shul* on Friday night (originally this stemmed from the fact that the site of services was also the building in which some took their Friday night meal). All the little children in synagogue scurry to line up in back of the person saying *Kiddush*, for they will each get a small cup of wine (or grape juice) after the leader concludes the prayer with a blessing over "the fruits of the vine." The services end with the singing of "*Yigdal Elokim Chai*" ("Exalted be the Living

God"), whose text is Maimonides' "Thirteen Principles of Faith." We sing *"Yigdal"* with gusto and appreciation for the Shabbat that is now upon us and the meal that awaits us. But what is this that we are singing? The sharpest articulation of dogma: affirmations about God's omniscience, omnipresence, omnipotence, and about the ultimate appearance of the Messiah and the resurrection of the dead! Do we not at least hesitate to sing out our belief in some of the "Thirteen Principles"? No, for in *shul* on Friday night "The Thirteen Principles of Faith" become *"Yigdal,"* a song of joyous thanksgiving for the Shabbat. (Of course, when one does come to reflect upon the faith of a Jew, the words of *"Yigdal"* will echo in one's mind and have to be dealt with.) As the services end we notice that we are breathing more deeply and freely than when we first arrived. We rise to shake hands and embrace one another. Shabbat is here.

I usually rush off soon after *shul*. Some folks stay and *schmooze* for a while. This is the time to catch up on the week of one's neighbor (some initiate this process a good deal earlier in the evening and continue it throughout services). Chances are that one has not seen him or her for the entire week: "If *you* thought *you* had a week, wait until I tell you about mine." As I walk briskly home I look at the heavens above. Though there are cars whizzing about me, the stars seem to know that it is Shabbat, the day that finalized all of creation.

"Shabbat Shalom" I call as I walk into my house. Nathan, my two-year-old comes toddling up to me, and Sarah, holding our infant Rebecca, follows. We all kiss "Shabbat Shalom" and go to the table--the table that has now been transformed by my wife into the Shabbes table: Our china is out, my silver *becher* (cup) is filled to the brim with red sweet wine, and underneath an embroidered cloth I can make out the two humps of our *challot* (Shabbat bread). In short, our home is now completely *Shabbesdik* (Sabbath-like).

We all sing "*Shalom Aleychem*," welcoming and blessing the angels who have come down to join us at our Shabbat table. This song, and the one that follows, gives one an opportunity to reflect upon the richness of one's family. As I sing I look around at Sarah, Nathan, and Rebecca and realize that I am truly blessed. The music underscores this feeling, or rather, it helps awaken it (much like background music on a television program lets viewers know that a scene evoking love is in progress). Indeed, music is the most articulate means we have of *expressing* emotion. I am reminded of the importance of song whenever I look into my baby Rebecca's eyes. It is just about impossible for me to look at Rebecca without singing something. So much love wells up inside of me that I must express it somehow. The tradition thus tells us that Shabbat is a time for song both to allow for the expression of joy, and to teach us that Shabbat *is*--and ought to be--a day of joy. The next song, "*Eishet Chayil*" ("An Accomplished Woman," Prov. 31.10-31), is sometimes only sung by the husband to his wife. In our family we all sing it in honor of all the women who are important to us. After the songs, my wife and I each bless our children, physically expressing what we have been feeling through the songs. We ask that Nathan be as righteous as the patriarchs and Rebecca as kind as the matriarchs of our people, and close each blessing with kisses and "*Yevarechecha ha-Shem ve-yishmerecha . . .*": "May God bless you and safeguard you . . ." (Num. 6.24-26).

All day the house has *smelled* of Shabbat and we are now to taste what has excited our appetites. First comes the *Kiddush* over the wine. As soon as I raise the wine cup Nathan begins to squirm, and stretches out his arm. He knows that he is about to taste the sweet red wine. Under Nathan's urging I hurry through the *Kiddush*, but we do manage, as do most families, to sing the verse "*ki vanu vacharta mi-kol ha'amim*": "For us did You choose and us did You sanctify from all the nations" (*Siddur* 361). It is important to realize the difference between the theological importance of this verse and the way it is experienced in the lives of many Jews. This verse, of course, is an exclamation of the doctrine of chosenness. Yet when one grows up *singing* this verse as a little ditty (it is not the most sophisticated or engrossing of melodies) before one understands the meaning of its words, what one comes to see expressed in song here is not pompous superiority, but an awareness of the rich feeling one gets from standing around the Shabbat table, looking at loved ones, smelling the delicious foods warming in the oven, watching the Shabbat candles dance before one's eyes. If one is to put this feeling in words it is one of thankfulness--not conceit. Theology here cannot be disengaged from praxis. The way Jews come to *think* of this verse cannot be isolated from the way Jews *experience* it in their lives.

We go now to wash our hands. This is a ritual washing before the eating of bread. I lift Nathan up, pour some water over his hands, then on my own, take a towel and we say: "*Baruch atah ha-Shem elokeynu melech ha'olam asher kiddishanu be-mitsvotav ve-tsivanu al netilat yadayim*": "Blessed are You God, King of the universe, Who has sanctified us with His commandments and has commanded us regarding washing the hands." There is no talking allowed in between this blessing and until after one has taken a bite of *challah*. I never thought of this as anything remarkable until we began inviting guests over who were not familiar with the traditional Shabbat. And it struck me that there are very few times outside of a religious ritual experience when a person *would* impose silence upon himself or herself. Of course, we all go to concerts or movies where we are supposed to be quiet, but there the restriction is not absolute (if I feel like I have something of interest to convey to my companion I do so quietly). Even if one is particularly scrupulous about being silent at a concert, however, there is quite an obvious reason for the silence: the desire not to disturb someone else's enjoyment of the performance. Why the silence here? By abstaining from talk before the blessing over the *challah* one is able to concentrate all one's attention on what is to come: the blessing, the *challah*, the meal. Indeed, the blessing over bread carries such weight that it obviates the need to individually bless each of the foods that come as part of the meal; it is a grace for the entire meal to come. The silence itself, then, focuses one's attention upon the experience of initiating a meal.

Sarah uncovers the *challot*, places one on top of the other and blesses God "Who has brought forth bread from the land." She then distributes a piece to each person at the table. Nathan loves the soft, fresh *challah* and Rebecca has just begun to enjoy it. This is a time to eat bread--just bread. Bread, that basic human food, is allowed sole control of our mouths for a few moments. We take our time chewing it; it feels good to eat again. We are fortunate. Sarah and I each gather a child up into our arms, go upstairs, and gently place Rebecca and Nathan down into their cribs. We softly say the first paragraph of the *Sh'ma* (Deut. 6.4-9), and kiss each child goodnight. Then we tiptoe out of the room, close the door, and return downstairs to an uninterrupted Shabbat meal.[4]

Different families have different traditional foods to eat on the Shabbat. Amongst the likely candidates for a Friday night meal are gefilte fish, chicken soup, chicken, kugels, salads, fruit, cake, and tea. Usually the time of year will dictate what is eaten and who is at one's table. In the summer, when the days are long and one does not sit down to the meal till after eight o'clock, the Friday night meal might be lighter than in the winter when it is eaten as early as six. If one reserves one big meal for family and one for guests, the summer noon meals (given the long day) will be the ones designated for guests. Food tastes extra special on Shabbat. Besides the fact that extra time is spent in the preparation of more elaborate meals than any other day of the week, there is also a physiological explanation for the

---

[4]If it has not been clear until now, the reader here will surely recognize that I write of a truly *Shabbesdik* Shabbes--where all goes well.

heightened sense of taste on the Sabbath. Warming of foods is allowed on Shabbat, but all cooking and baking must end by Friday sundown. Because of this, when one comes to the meal on Friday night the smells of what one is about to eat have been percolating throughout the house, tantalizing one's appetite. Add to this the custom of intentionally coming to the Shabbat table a bit hungrier than to a normal meal, and one is powerfully predisposed to enjoy whatever foods are served.

Ideally, the sounds at the Shabbat table should be replete with those of *divrei Torah* (words of Torah) and *zemirot* (songs). I do not limit the concept of *divrei Torah* to Judaica, but extend it to all branches of inquiry pertinent to the Jewish civilization--from history to politics to economics to literature. There is to be a certain *kedushah* (holiness) at the Shabbat table. One should be able to tell the difference between a recording of a family's conversation during a Thursday night dinner and that same family's talk on Friday night. (Of course, a main difference will be that everyone in the family who is living at home will make it their business to attend the Friday meal). Even more than usual, at the Shabbat table I try to refrain from *lashon hara'* (gossip), and try to restrain my family from it. It is amazing to realize how much of our conversations come down to our talking (often disapprovingly) about other people. Ultimately what these conversations are about is the attempt to say "I am better than so and so." What is there to talk about if this huge chunk of conversation disappears? Are we each valuable in ourselves? It is up to every family to discover this for itself.

When in American life do families get together and sing? Religious families, to be sure, will often join in congregational singing in churches or synagogues, but there is something to be said for singing *zemirot* with just one's family. Each person hears his or her own voice and their loved ones' clearly, as all touch each other through song. My wife and I have often been guests in families' homes where elaborate meals are served, but where no songs are sung. This is a pity. The spirit of Shabbat resides in song. How better to experience the *neshamah yeterah*, the extra soul, than by a song? When I sing I feel more than I think. Music articulates feeling in a way that words cannot. That is why the *zemirot* repertoire need not be large, and that is the reason for wordless Chassidic melodies called *nigunim*. Singing actualizes the love present at a Shabbat table. Opening oneself up to song, one opens up to a life of feeling.

The meal concludes with a long grace after meals--all of it sung. Again, depending on the time of year this may mark the conclusion of the evening's activities. For Shabbat *is* a time to rest. Many people look forward to Friday night as the night that they know they can be in bed by ten o'clock. And surprisingly, one is utterly exhausted by ten. It seems that the body has a way of regulating expenditures of energy. Wednesday night at ten I might be sorting laundry in front of the television set. Friday night at ten I cannot keep my eyes open. Indeed, there are many people who go to bed a good deal earlier than ten o'clock on Friday night--often sleeping for twelve hours--making up for sleep deprivation during the week. The body, of course, needs sleep. Shabbat gives the body an opportunity for sleep. People might think that they want to go partying every Friday night, but Shabbat tells them that they are tired, that they need a good night's sleep.

The custom of reserving Friday night for lovemaking is often remarked upon.[5] The truth of the matter is that during the summer months when Friday night meals are late and Shabbat afternoons are long, the afternoons are better suited for making love.[6] In any case there is a good bit of wisdom in emphasizing sexual activity on Shabbat. The reason is time: Shabbat allows a couple time for intimacy--not just orgasm. That is, it is quite

---

[5]See, for example, Irving Greenberg, "The Dream and How to Live It: Shabbat," *The Jewish Way: Living the Holidays* (New York: Summit, 1988) 141, 173.

[6]I depart from rabbinic Judaism here. According to halachah (Jewish law), lovemaking is restricted to the darkness of night-time.

possible for a couple to turn off the nightly news and then make love to each partners' sexual satisfaction. But it takes more than ten minutes to touch the one you love. This touching need not always be tactile--there is no hurry on Shabbat to manually stimulate each others' erogenous zones to produce the requisite results. Quiet talk can be part of intimacy. Embraces can be allowed to last. See, there is nothing *to do* on Shabbat--no television, movies, bars, concerts, ballet. But one discovers that there are things worthwhile that do not involve those activities.

PART II

THE RELIGIOUS LIFE AS ARTFUL EXPERIENCE

CHAPTER 5

THE STRATEGY OF "THE RELIGIOUS LIFE AS ARTFUL EXPERIENCE"

In Part I I explored one way of thinking about the religious life that could serve to sustain religious commitment. The idea of religion as an anthropological necessity can act to assuage any doubts a person might have as to the rational justification for leading a traditional religious life. In this part of the work I derive a strategy from the nature of religious experience itself. However, **the religious life as artful experience**--the strategy for sustaining religious commitment to emerge from my work here--will not be fully affective or effective as "idea." The *idea* of the religious life as artful experience can only be fully realized, as we will see, when it is affectively presented, when it is made to be self-involving. This strategy requires argument and demonstration: the argument as to the nature of religious experience, and rich depiction of the religious life. In this chapter I make this argument by examining the nature of religious experience; in the following chapter I draw upon the work of Abraham Heschel--the most affective modern Jewish theologian--to demonstrate that Heschel's power lies precisely in his ability to write affective theology. At the end of this part (as at the end of Part I), I offer what this strategy mandates for each individual: a personal affectional depiction of one's own religious life. In this way I demonstrate how religious living can be artful living. I also constructively bolster my argument that, in a society dominated by the rationalism of the cultured despisers of religion, the religious way of life must be affectively depicted if it is to be persuasive and intelligible.

Religious Experience and the Human Being

The nature of religious experience is difficult to ascertain. It is possible to know much about the history of a particular religion and little about the experiencing of that religion. Mircea Eliade makes this point concisely when he writes that "the historicity of a religious experience does not tell us what a religious experience ultimately *is*. We know that we can grasp the sacred only through manifestations which are always historically conditioned. But the study of these historically conditioned expressions does not give us the answer to the questions: What is the sacred? What does a religious experience actually mean?"[1] As a preliminary step in answering these questions we turn to consider the nature of the human being that religious experience expresses. In doing so we are repeating a venture begun in Part I--searching for the humanness of the human being. What unites the writers to be cited here is a sense that the nature of the human being can only be "settled" with a rather unsettling word: "mystery." This proves to be the only word to "explain" the inexplicable: why and how human beings are able--often with complete disregard of their rational inclinations--to be kind, cruel, giving, sadistic, vengeful, murderous, apathetic, caring, and loving.

Abraham Joshua Heschel is the theologian *par excellence* to stress the wonder and the mystery of the human: "The search of reason ends at the shore of the known; on the immense expanse beyond it only the sense of the ineffable can glide"; "Wonder rather than doubt is the root of knowledge"; "We may doubt anything except that we are struck with amazement"; "The most incomprehensible fact is the fact that we can comprehend at all."[2] The human being is supra-rational--it transcends rational existence (as Heschel says, "reasoning is not the only motor of mental life," MNA 15). The human

---

[1] Mircea Eliade, *The Quest: History and Meaning in Religion* (Chicago: The Univ. of Chicago Press, 1969) 53. Henceforth cited by page alone.

[2] Abraham Joshua Heschel, *Man is Not Alone: A Philosophy of Religion*, 1951 (New York: Farrar, Straus & Giroux, 1988) 7, 11, 13. Henceforth cited as MNA by page alone.

being's rational ability itself is a reflection of the wonder of being human. Echoing the work of Heschel from a Catholic perspective is Nicholas Lash: "The man who finds it easy to speak of God, or the ways of God with man, is the man whose mind and heart are not sufficiently open to the mystery to be dazzled and silenced by it. The discourse of the man who does not know that the human is profoundly mysterious is as superficial, as lacking in seriousness, as is the discourse of the man who finds it easy to talk about God."[3] Lash, like Heschel, begins with the mystery of the human, with a sense of radical amazement at life. To be human is to be struck with wonder--and to *know* that one is struck with wonder. Both Lash and Heschel point to the indigenous reality of self-transcendence through human awareness. Transcendent feelings of wonder and amazement are brought about by the human being's capacity to be aware of itself.

Psychology also teaches about the mystery of the human being. Erich Fromm writes that "while life in its merely biological aspects is a miracle and a secret, man in his human aspects is an unfathomable secret to himself--and to his fellow man. We know ourselves, and yet even with all the efforts we may make, we do not know ourselves."[4] And William James writes that "if we look on man's whole mental life as it exists, we have to confess that the part of it of which rationalism can give an account is relatively superficial. The truth is that in the metaphysical and religious sphere, articulate reasons are cogent for us only when our inarticulate feelings of reality have already been impressed in favor of the same conclusion."[5] The human being as the thinking animal only delimits the areas of existence that are amenable to rational appropriation--it cannot "explain" the human itself psychologically or

---

[3]Nicholas Lash, *Voices of Authority* (Shepherdstown: Patmos, 1976) 106.
[4]Erich Fromm, *The Art of Loving*, 1956 (New York: Harper & Row, 1974) 24. Henceforth cited by page alone.
[5]William James, *The Varieties of Religious Experience: A Study in Human Nature*, 1902 (New York: NAL Penguin, 1958) 72. Henceforth cited by page alone.

biologically.

James, furthermore, articulates the limits of rationality. He argues that in "the metaphysical and religious sphere" what is reasonable will directly depend on one's affective predisposition. A contemporary scholar, Margaret Farley, emphasizes this point when she writes that "We choose no commitments to which we are totally indifferent. We deliberate about choosing only commitments which are in some way related to the already actualized structure of our affectivity. Commitments-to-be-chosen, then, emerge as possible objects of choice only because they are already in some way related to some dimension of our life-process."[6] Farley feels no need to limit her statement to "the metaphysical and religious sphere." She argues that all commitments entail a certain predisposition to that commitment. We can extend Farley's work and say that, ordinarily, to have an experience is to be predisposed to absorb that experience--even in the realm of science. For example, if one wants to learn from a book on applied mathematics one has to: a) be able to read the language of the text; and b) understand what constitutes a "proof." Similarly, as James also indicates, a faith commitment to a particular religious tradition will depend on whether or not one is affectively predisposed to that tradition. Here again the emotional life of the human being sets the stage for its rational operations.

Reason is grounded by one's affective predispositions to reason. Human story-telling and myth-making explore precisely this idea--when and how human beings act in ways that supersede their rational intuitions. As Philip Roth once remarked: "I seem to be interested in how--and why and when--a man acts counter to what he considers to be his 'best self,' or what others assume it to be, or would like it to be. The subject is hardly 'mine';

---

[6]Margaret A. Farley, *A Study in the Ethics of Commitment within the Context of Theories of Human Love and Temporality*, diss., Yale University, 1974, 280. Farley continues her study of commitment in her recent book, *Personal Commitments: Beginning, Keeping, Changing* (San Francisco: Harper & Row, 1986).

it interested readers and writers for a long time before it became my turn to be engaged by it too."[7] Henri Bergson also draws attention to this quality of the human: "To connect religion with a system of ideas, with a logic or a 'pre-logic,' is to turn our remote ancestors into intellectuals, and intellectuals such as we ought to be in greater numbers ourselves, for we often see the finest theories succumbing to passion and interest and holding good only in our hours of speculative thought, whereas ancient religions pervaded the whole of life. The truth is that religion, being co-extensive with our species, must pertain to our structure."[8] Like Roth, Bergson notes the tendency of the human being to be more passionate than rational. He connects this passional tendency with what it is to be human, adducing from the fact that "ancient religion pervaded the whole of life" the corollary that religion is less a system of ideas and more a way of acting and feeling--and that this quality "pertains to our structure." Religion is an expression of the human being and not an expression of the rational ideas of the human being.

As to the nature of this "human being," Bergson highlights the fact that the human being "is alone in realizing that he is subject to illness, alone in knowing that he must die. . . . Of all the creatures that live in society, man alone can swerve from the social line by giving way to selfish preoccupations when the common good is at stake; in all other societies the interests of the individual are inexorably co-ordinate with and subordinate to the general interest. This twofold shortcoming in man is the price paid for intelligence" (194). Bergson thus points out that the natural existence of

---

[7]Philip Roth, "Writing About Jews," 1963, *Reading Myself and Others* (New York: Farrar, Straus and Giroux, 1975) 152. Roth puts the word "mine" in quotations because he is defending his decision to tell the story of an adulterous Jewish man in "Epstein." Roth argues that while the particular story is his own, the broad subject is not. Thus, no malicious or antisemitic intent can be ascribed to the writer of such a story as "Epstein."

[8]Henri Bergson, *The Two Sources of Morality and Religion*, 1932, trans. R. Ashley Audra and Cloudesley Brereton (New York: H. Holt and Co., 1935) 166. Henceforth cited by page alone.

intelligence brings with it a natural liability of disorder, dis-ease, and social anarchy. But he argues that "the myth-making function, which belongs to intelligence . . . is a defensive reaction of nature against what might be depressing for the individual, and dissolvent for society, in the exercise of intelligence" (194). Bergson here adds to what we have already learned about the emotional life predisposing the rational. He argues that the uniqueness of the human in the realm of the emotions lies in the fact that *the human being is the self-reflexive feeling animal.* (Erich Fromm, similarly, speaks of the human being as *"life being aware of itself,"* 6.) That is, while other animals experience pain, joy, loneliness, and other emotional states, only the human being can reflect upon these states and be *aware* of pain, passion, joy, and sadness.

Bergson says that because of the human being's self-reflexivity, the passion to live can be impaired. Religion thus becomes a way for rational beings to preserve their passion for life: "Religion is that element which, in beings endowed with reason, is called upon to make good any deficiency to attachment to life" (199). The way religion can correct this "deficiency" is to express what it means to be alive, to articulate the wonder of living. And the way the human being characteristically comes to express this wonder of the human takes artistic and/or religious forms. Since we already know that a life patterned after these forms will affectively predispose a person to think, feel, and believe in a certain way, we are now in a position to combine what we have learned so far and say: *Religious experience expresses the wonder of being the self-reflexive feeling animal, and predisposes an individual to certain intellectual propositions, emotional attitudes, and transcendent beliefs.*

Religion begins, then, with the mystery of life, with the mystery of the human being. But of course, "to begin" is to seek to penetrate that mystery, and it is to inevitably accept some presuppositions as "true." What are these presuppositions about human life? For our purposes there are two. The first is, to quote from Miguel de Unamuno, that "*the end of life is living and not understanding.*"[9] Bergson also stresses this point: "Before any man can philosophize he must live" (154). The second presupposition (again quoting Unamuno) is that "*What I feel is a truth,* at any rate as much a truth as what I see, touch, hear, or what is demonstrated to me" (116, emphasis added). What is immediately clear from these presuppositions is that feeling is to be included with "true" living. But what is living? Here we come to the importance of the religious life, for many religions lay down prescriptions for right living. Life lived according to a Way enables a person to actualize his or her being: "The only way in which the world can be grasped ultimately lies, not in thought, but in the act, in the experience of oneness" (Fromm 65).[10] To be human is to live; to be religious is to consciously live a certain Way.

Both of the presuppositions here mitigate intellectualism in the experiencing of life. Living, to be sure, does not exclude understanding, but it sets the parameters for it. Within the religious sphere itself, living must also precede understanding. James sought to demonstrate this in his major work, *The Varieties of Religious Experience*. In answering his own rhetorical question as to "why I have been so bent on rehabilitating the element of feeling in religion and subordinating its intellectual part," James says that "individuality is founded in feeling; and the recesses of feeling, the darker, blinder strata of character, are the only places in the world in which we catch real fact in the making, and directly perceive how events happen, and how work is actually done" (379). James is directly in keeping with our second presupposition, that "what I feel is a truth," and implies here that "real fact

[9]Miguel de Unamuno, *The Tragic Sense of Life in Man and in Peoples*, trans. J. E. Crawford Flitch, 1921 (London: Macmillan and Co., 1926) 116, emphasis added. Henceforth cited by page alone.
[10]Fromm argues that this "experience of oneness" is the end of all human endeavor. He writes that "Man--of all ages and cultures--is confronted with the solution of one and the same question: the question of how to overcome separateness, how to achieve union, how to transcend one's own individual life and find at-onement" (8).

in the making" lies mainly in feeling--not in thought.

If religion is to give the human being access to the mystery of life, religious truth will be most closely akin to felt experience and less to intellectual doctrines. As David Tracy asserts: "Truth, in its primordial sense, is manifestation." He writes that "anyone who has experienced even one such moment [of truth]--in watching a film, in listening to music, in looking at a painting, in participating in a religious ritual, in reading a classic text, in conversation with friends, or in finding oneself in love--knows that truth as manifestation is real."[11] It is no coincidence that Tracy evokes film, music, painting, literature, friendship, and love as moments of the manifestation of truth rather than, say, the moment when one grasps a mathematical formula. Tracy speaks of moments of transcendent truths, of moments when one feels in passionate synchrony with what is being expressed. It is helpful to think of all these forms of expression--including ritual, friendship, and love--as art. (Significantly, Fromm calls his book *The Art of Loving*.) Art, taken in its widest sense, is the ability to express life--life whose end is living rather than understanding, life where "what I feel" is true, and where the truth about what I feel is the truth to be expressed.[12]

Art, Ritual, Play

Human beings tend to express their lives in what Susanne Langer calls "living form," which she says is "the most indubitable product of all good art. Such form is 'living' in that it . . . *expresses* life--feeling, growth, movement, emotion, and everything that characterizes vital existence."[13] Indeed, Langer

---

[11]David Tracy, *Plurality and Ambiguity: Hermeneutics, Religion, Hope* (San Francisco: Harper & Row, 1987) 29. Henceforth cited by page alone.

[12]Not every work of art is perceived to express truth, though every work of art expresses feeling (I discuss this, using Susanne Langer's work, in the following section). I use "art" to denote works whose affect strikes one as true. In this essay I am particularly concerned with the art of theological writing--how it is perceived to be true.

[13]Susanne Langer, *Feeling And Form: A Theory of Art Developed from* Philosophy in a New Key (New York: Charles Scribner's Sons, 1953) 82. Henceforth cited as FF by page alone.

finds that "expression in the logical sense--presentation of an idea through an articulate symbol--is the ruling power and purpose of art" (FF 67). She thus comes to speak of art as *virtual* ("created only for perception," 107) expression. The art of painting, for example, expresses virtual space; the art of music, virtual time; poesis, virtual life. Drawing upon what we have learned from Unamuno we can say here that art is the human being's way of *expressing* that "the end of life is living." Art is able to create virtual human experience. Art is able to convey what it is to be alive.

Why is art virtual expression? Because art, says Langer, is "the creation of form expressive of human feeling" (FF 60). Again, Langer's work can be buttressed by reference to Unamuno. Art's importance in the human enterprise is suggested by Unamuno's inclusion of feeling as part of true experience. If "what I feel is a truth," then the creation of "form expressive of human feeling" will be important to my existence. Of course, this does not address the question of *how* art is able to do this. Why is art particularly expressive of human feeling? The answer to this question lies in the non-discursive nature of artistic expression. Langer writes that non-discursive form in art can "articulate knowledge that cannot be rendered discursively because it concerns experiences that are not *formally* amenable to the discursive projection" (240). The "knowledge" that Langer speaks of here is that of feeling. She thus writes: "More than anything else in experience, the arts mold our actual life of feeling. . . Artistic training is, therefore, the education of feeling, as our usual schooling in factual subjects, and logical skills . . . is the education of thought" (401). Simply put, art and feeling share a common non-discursive form. Art is therefore able to articulate feeling in a way that discursive form cannot. To be schooled in art is to open oneself up to a life of feeling--and to do this is to live.

Before modernity, one implicitly experienced ritual as art. Art and religion thrive together and strengthen one another in a society in which there is just one claim to ultimacy (a society where religion does not need to construct "plausibility structures"). Art in this situation expresses characteristic feelings of responding to ultimacy (whether these be feelings of dependence, joy, happiness, awe, etc.). In fact, says Langer, "when religious imagination is the dominant force in society, art is scarcely separable from it. . . ." The reason for this, she argues, is that "art does not affect the viability of life so much as its quality; that, however, it affects profoundly. In this way it is akin to religion, which also, at least in its pristine, vigorous, spontaneous phase, defines and develops human feelings" (FF 402). As religion loses its hold upon people's feelings, as religion comes to compete with other claims of ultimacy for people's feelings, art is freed to express human responses to the new dominant societal forces. As a result of this, two things happen to the detriment of both religion and art: art loses "its traditional sphere of influence, the solemn, festive populace, and runs the danger of never reaching beyond the studio where it was created" (FF 402), and religion comes to be thought of as static rather than as dynamic human creation. So if we now say that ritual is art or that ritual can be art, meaning that ritual can be "symbolic of human feeling," we are not naively trying to turn back the clock on modernity. We are arguing that the form already exists with which to creatively express one's emotional life--the form of ritual. **The religious life as artful experience** argues for this view of the religious life as defining and developing complex human feelings. It builds upon Langer's claim that "a rite regularly performed is the constant reiteration of sentiments toward first and last things" (PNK 134). **Religion as artful experience** shows how religious ritual evokes attitudes and emotions appropriate to the mystery of existence. It asserts that the power of ritual can still be discovered in a postmodern pluralistic setting, for though art and religion have become divorced in our society--so that one goes to a museum for art, and to a church or synagogue for religion--the emotional lives of human beings still take characteristically non-discursive forms of expression.

But if ritual is indeed artful why is it any better than any other art form? This is a thorny issue that must be addressed, for in our consumer society one has to justify spending two hours at a church or synagogue, but one does not have to do so for two hours spent in a theater or symphony.[14] Worship (and other rituals) must be defended against the "cultured despisers'" charge of wasting time, while an evening of opera--where one is also not "producing" anything tangible--is presumed to be a worthwhile experience. We seem to recognize the emotional importance of participating in "high culture," but we are rather ignorant of the emotional significance of ritual. Here the strategy of depicting and perceiving the religious life as artful experience comes into play. It articulates in the sphere of religion what we intuitively grasp of the experience of "high cultural forms": that human creativity marks us as feeling beings--remembering here that to be human is to be self-reflexive about one's feelings.

In considering the affective power of art, one sees that artful experience will be most affective when it is practiced as ritual. As Langer notices, part of ritual's power comes from the fact that it is "a disciplined rehearsal of right attitudes" (PNK 134). Without discipline there is no art or mastery of art. Fromm remarks that "aside from learning the theory and practice, there is a third factor necessary to becoming a master in any art--the mastery of the art must be a matter of ultimate concern; there must be nothing else in the world more important than the art. This holds true for music, for medicine, for carpentry--and for love" (4-5). We also include "religion" here as well. **Religion as artful experience** requires mastery as art. The point therefore is not that religion is a good alternative to art, but that

---

[14]Significantly, too, a shopping trip that results in no purchases is not usually looked upon as wasted time. The act of shopping has implicitly been elevated to an art; the experience itself is felt to be valuable.

the religious life can come to be artful experience. If this strategy is articulated and expressed affectively not only will it be powerful for sustaining religious commitment (through the "lure of feeling" as Whitehead says),[15] but it will shift our discourse of the religious life away from justification and toward appreciation. This in turn will prove more affective and effective in sustaining religious commitment, as dead rituals--rituals that no longer are expressive of human feelings--come to be replaced by vibrant, vital ones.

Thinking about the religious life as artful experience has the further advantage of highlighting the importance of action in religious life. Like art, religion requires *practice*. In focusing upon religious activity we get at the consequence of religion for human beings. The religious life has long been a part of human existence because it expresses what it means to be alive--and "the end of life is living and not understanding." To concentrate upon the religious life as *thought* is, according to Bergson, to "historize" religion, for he argues:

> History is knowledge, religion is mainly action: it concerns knowledge, as we have repeated over and over again, only in so far as an intellectual representation is needed to ward off the dangers of a certain intellectuality. To consider this representation apart, to criticize it *as* a representation, would be to forget that it forms an amalgam with the accompanying action. We commit just such an error when we ask ourselves how it is that great minds can have accepted the tissue of childish imaginings, nay absurdities, which made up their religion. The movements of a swimmer would appear just as silly and ridiculous to anyone forgetting that the water is there, that this water sustains the swimmer, and that the man's movements, the resistance of the liquid, the current of the river, must be taken all together as an undivided whole. (190)[16]

---

[15]Langer borrows this phrase from Whitehead in *Feeling And Form* 397.

[16]Heschel also provides a vivid image to support the claim that ritual action cannot be viewed in isolation. He relates a story told by the modern founder of chassidism, the Ba'al Shem Tov ("Bearer of the Divine Name": Israel ben Eliezer, 1700-1760): "A musician was playing on a very beautiful instrument, and the music so enraptured the people that they were driven to dance ecstatically. Then a deaf man who knew nothing of music passed by, and seeing the enthusiastic dancing of the people he decided they must be insane. Had he

Bergson uses the art of swimming to reverse the way we usually think about the relation between thought and action in religion. For Bergson, it is not that "intellectual representations" or religious doctrines are expressed through ritual, but that ritual upholds the "intellectual representations" (as water does a swimmer). Doctrines only make sense when viewed in the larger religious spectrum. One might say that doctrines are the human being's negative defense mechanism against "any deficiency of attachment to life." Positive action in *affirming* "attachment to life" comes through ritual. Remember here that Mary Douglas argued that the efficacy of ritual is "achieved in the action itself, in the assertions it makes and the experience which bears its imprinting" (68). Ritual shapes, frames, and controls experience primarily through action. One affirms religious doctrines out of a context of a life of ritual, and one performs the ritual because one is alive. As Bergson emphatically notes: "We shall say it over and over again: before man can philosophize man must live" (166). And life is foremost not a life of abstract ideas, but a life of action and feeling. Put another way: meanings to emerge from ritual activity will be of the first-order of religious experience; meanings to emerge from doctrinal beliefs will be of the second-order of religious experience.

In modernity, a discussion of ritual must confront the dialectic between "practical purpose" and "meaning." The matter can be stated simply: can activity that has no apparent purpose be meaningful? Romano Guardini answers strongly in the affirmative: "Objects which have no purpose in the strict sense of the term have a meaning. This meaning is not realised by their extraneous effect or by the contribution which they make to the stability or the modification of another object, but their significance consists in being what they are. Measured by the strict sense of the word, they are purpose-

---

been wise he would have sensed their joy and rapture and joined their dancing" (*God In Search of Man* 249-250).

less, but still full of meaning."[17] Significantly, Guardini brings in the nature of art here: "The work of art has no purpose, but it has a meaning . . . that it should exist, and that it should clothe in clear and genuine form the essence of things and the inner life of the human artist" (91). One might say that art is meaningful because it *expresses* meaning. Through its non-discursiveness, art is able to communicate ideas of feeling. As Langer notes: "What art expresses is *not* actual feeling, but ideas of feeling; as language does not express actual things and events but ideas of them" (FF 59). These ideas will take different forms in the different media of art, and the resultant affect on the viewer/participant will reveal the meaning of a particular work of art. Here is the complementary notion to Peter Berger's claim that "society is the guardian of order and meaning not only objectively, in its institutional structures, but subjectively as well, in its structuring of individual consciousness" (21). For Berger, the meaning of an individual's action always emerges in *relation* to the structure of meaning in a society. Similarly, meanings do not reside *in* works of art, but are disclosed through the relation, the affect, of art on a viewer. There is relationality in artful experience.

Paradigmatic for Guardini as something that has no purpose but has meaning is play, and Guardini specifically develops the notion of play with regard to the (Catholic) liturgy.[18] He defines play as "life, pouring itself forth without an aim, seizing upon riches from its own abundant store, significant through the fact of its existence" (99). He writes that play characteristically manifests itself most readily in "the play of the child and the creation of the artist," and goes on to say:

---

[17]Romano Guardini, *The Spirit of the Liturgy*, trans. Ada Lane (London: Sheed & Ward, 1937) 90. Henceforth cited by page alone.

[18]I confine my analysis here to what Guardini has to say about the general effect of liturgy. It should be understood, however, that the specific mythos enacted and presented in each tradition's liturgy will necessarily contain its own affectional grammar.

> The child, when it plays, does not aim at anything. It has no purpose. It does not want to do anything but to exercise its youthful powers, pour forth its life in an aimless series of movements, words and actions, and by this to develop and to realise itself more fully: all of which is purposeless, but full of meaning nevertheless, the significance in the unchecked revelation of this youthful life in thoughts and words, movements and actions, in the capture and expression of its nature, and in the fact of its existence. (98)

If there is meaning to life itself, play expresses this meaning. If we are to say that a two-year-old is valuable in itself, then we are saying that this child *today* is valuable--and not just potentially valuable for whom it will *become*. And a two-year-old is a creature of play. Art expresses this truth. Art gives life to being and to the meaning of being alive.

Guardini notes that the liturgy in particular is the human being's chance for play--holy play. He says that in the liturgy the human being

> is given the opportunity of realising his fundamental essence, of really becoming that which according to his divine destiny he should be and longs to be, a child of God. . . . Because the life of the liturgy is higher than that to which customary reality gives both the opportunity and form of expression, it adopts suitable forms and methods from that sphere in which alone they are to be found, that is to say, from art. . . . [Liturgy] unites art and reality in a supernal childhood before God. . . . It has no purpose, but is full of profound meaning. It is not work, but play. To be at play, or to fashion a work of art in God's sight--not to create, but to exist-- such is the essence of the liturgy. (101-102)

Art, ritual, play all come together. The child expresses itself through the ritual of play. To be a child before God is to master the art of holy play by artfully manipulating symbolic forms to express the sanctity of life. Guardini in fact writes that the worshiper not only becomes an *artist* through the liturgy, but he or she also becomes a work of art: "The practice of the liturgy means that by the help of grace, under the guidance of the Church, we grow into living works of art before God, with no other aim or purpose than that of living and existing in His sight" (105). What emerges from Guardini, then, is the notion that ritual in general and liturgy in particular ought to be construed as holy play: "life pouring itself forth without an aim." Though this activity might have no practical purpose it has a meaning (that of existing in God's sight, for Guardini). What is created therefore in ritual is play, the emotional outpourings of the human being.[19] The physical trappings of the ritual are the symbolic forms that are manipulated to create virtual life--and life is living, life is feeling. Only in this sense can a given ritual form become expressive and artful because only through art does the human being come to *learn* what it is to feel. Of course every human being, as self-reflexive feeling animal, feels and knows that it feels, but if one wants an "education of feeling" one has to turn to art, to play, to ritual.

One learns from Guardini that ritual is holy play. Johan Huizinga, in *Homo Ludens: A Study of the Play-Element in Culture*, emphasizes the reverse of this equation and argues that play resembles the holy.[20] Like Guardini, Huizinga has to struggle against the prevalent denigration of play as childish and make-believe--and therefore frivolous and trifling: "We are accustomed to think of play and seriousness as an absolute antithesis. It would seem, however, that this does not go to the heart of the matter."[21] Huizinga explains:

---

[19]Precisely how ritual becomes holy play is a crucial concern of this book. I argue that this can only be discerned in the actual performance of ritual, and can be virtually experienced through rich, affective depictions of the religious life (as demonstrated by Chapters 4, 7, 8, and 10 of this work).

[20]Huizinga explicity refers to Guardini's work. He cites Guardini's reference to the liturgy as "pointless but significant," and traces this notion of holy play to Plato: "We characterize ritual as play. The ritual act has all the formal and essential characteristics of play ... particularly in so far as it transports the participants to another world. This identity of ritual and play was unreservedly recognized by Plato as a given fact [cf. *Laws* vii, 803] (Huizinga 18). Note that Huizinga's reference here to "another world" vividly recalls for us George Santayana's definition of religion: "Another world to live in--whether we expect ever to pass wholly into it or no--is what we mean by having a religion," *The Life of Reason* (New York: Charles Scribner's Sons, 1936) 5.

[21]Johan Huizinga, *Homo Ludens: A Study of the Play-Element in Culture* (New York: Roy Publishers, 1950) 18. Henceforth cited by page alone.

> In play as we conceive it the distinction between belief and make-believe breaks down. The concept of play merges quite naturally with that of holiness. . . . Primitive, or let us say, archaic ritual is thus sacred play, indispensable for the well-being of the community, fecund of cosmic insight and social development but always play in the sense Plato gave to it--an action accomplishing itself outside and above the necessities and seriousness of everyday life. In this sphere of sacred play the child and the poet are at home with the savage. (25)

Huizinga implies that when a person--child or adult--truly plays, that person is enveloped in a world of play that has its own demands and goals. Often, say in tennis where two players are of equal physical skills, it is precisely this ability of a person to completely enter the world of play that is the decisive difference in the outcome of the match. This is why athletes are told to concentrate, to focus their attention on the immediate task at hand (such as hitting a tennis ball): a person who thinks about an upcoming dinner engagement when he or she plays a point will not do as well as someone who concentrates on (we might say "attends to") the ball. Indeed, this is why some athletes find it helpful to go through ritual actions at certain moments in their sports that demand a great deal of concentration. These moments can be found in various sports; they occur at precisely those times when play is stopped and must be started again. In tennis, this moment comes at the start of a tennis serve (in basketball, it is at the free-throw line; in baseball, it is both for the pitcher about to throw and for the batter about to swing). Players will usually bounce the service ball a ritualized number of times, for example. This *action* allows the player to remain focused within the world of tennis, disengaging his or her mind from thinking about the perils of a double fault. One might say (in light of the religious anthropologists) that the ritual of bouncing the tennis ball controls the experience of the serve. Force a player to bounce the ball three times instead of a ritualized four times and his or her service game rapidly deteriorates.

Ritual action performs a similar function in religious play. The action allows a person to remain in a world where life itself is being expressed. That Huizinga limited sacred play to "archaic ritual" is an indication that in our pluralistic society of multiple claims to ultimacy it is rare for a person to become wholly engaged in belief and enter the world of ritual.[22] In modern secular consumer societies ritual activity is not fully attended to; one is constantly tempted to interrupt ritual action with the question of "Why am I doing this?" because the activity does not involve what the society values most: the accumulation of goods or capital.[23] Even if one comes up with a satisfying answer to the question, however, the ritual play has already lost much of its vitality. It becomes more of a hobby than an expression of one's life.

In his chapter on "Play-Forms in Art" Huizinga, like many other writers,[24] points to the particular affective and play-ful quality of music: "Our civilization is worn with age and too sophisticated. But nothing helps us to regain that sense so much as musical sensibility. In feeling music we feel ritual. In the enjoyment of music, whether it is meant to express religious ideas or not, the perception of the beautiful and the sensation of holiness merge, and the distinction between play and seriousness is whelmed in that fusion" (158). We might clarify Huizinga's statement here by saying

---

[22]It is also probably true that Huizinga, like Bergson and Langer, tended to speak of religious ritual in its "pristine" or "archaic" form only--as if religion's vital function can never be recaptured. In this they are part of the "cultured despisers'" tradition. They imply that modern human beings are post-religious, and (even if religion once had a vital role to play) one cannot and should not try to turn back the clock on modernity. The strategies for sustaining religious commitment developed in this work argue that while civilization changes, the nature of the human being remains the same--and it is this nature that religion has always sought to express.

[23]Significantly, the importance ascribed to an athletic event in our society directly depends upon how much money is ventured on its outcome. The more money at stake, the "bigger" the game.

[24]Schleiermacher, one of the first modern religious writers to emphasize the religious affections, also noted religion's kinship with music: "Were I to compare religion in this respect with anything it would be with music, which indeed is otherwise closely connected with it" (*On Religion* 51).

that "in feeling music we learn of what it is to feel ritual." Music, that ethereal intangible, is for many the most articulate of forms to convey human emotions and passions. Langer expresses this idea clearly when she writes: "Music articulates forms which language cannot set forth. Art is formally and essentially untranslatable because the form of human feelings are much more congruent with musical forms than with the forms of language; music can *reveal* the nature of feelings with a detail and truth that language cannot approach" (PNK 198-199). It is no wonder that worship has traditionally been accompanied by music. Music has the ability to speak directly to one's emotions. When a somber piece of music accompanies a penitential prayer, for example, one is readily able to *feel* penitential. But one can feel ritual even when music is not an integral element of the ritual. One simply has to be at-tuned to the symphony of life, to the fact of ritual as life pouring itself out into symbolic forms.

What emerges from Langer, Huizinga, and Guardini, therefore, is that art is not a "vacation" from life, but has the particular ability to express feelings that are focused on significant features of existence. We have learned to think of ritual as artful play in that it bears all the hallmarks of life expressing itself. If we now come to our strategy of viewing the religious life as artful experience, we can say that to perform a particular ritual gives one access to the creation of a virtual experience and--within the scope of a complex ritual system--to the "clarification of one's emotional life" (FF 409). To utilize **religion as artful experience**, then, is to use the culturally accepted term "art" as a strategy for sustaining religious commitment by attending fully to one's own ritual life, and by seeing how ritual expresses feeling. With the realization of **the religious life as artful experience,** one will be in a position to judge whether the feelings expressed in that experience bespeak the holy, whether one is (also) acting in God's sight.

Why we would want to employ **religion as artful experience** is clear:

98

if we are able to think of the religious life as an artful one, our general cultural milieu can be used to deepen our religious commitment.[25] The *justification* for working out this strategy can be argued discursively, as was done in this chapter. Religion was linked to art (and play) through its ritualized action, whereby meanings are disclosed affectively. Ultimately, however, the proof for this strategy is revealed in precisely the non-discursive realm of art. Only when one experiences the emotional depth of ritual can one's life become a work of art. Through a complete ritual system--which ritualizes the many activities of the human being--every human action can be elevated to the realm of art. In Judaism one would speak here of raising all aspects of life to the level of *kedushah* (holiness). One learns in the traditional Jewish way of life, for example, about the *kedushah* of the body: there is an art to eating (and there is an art to preparing the food to be eaten), there is even an art to excreting, and there is an art to making love. One learns also of the *kedushah* of the "other": there is an art to conducting one's business affairs, there is an art to giving charity, and there is an art to pursuing peace.

While **the religious life as artful experience** draws upon the position of art in our society, it cannot be persuasive unless it artfully presents the religious life. As artful experience the religious life must compete for attention the way all art does--affectively. An affective presentation of religion, whether through word, sounds, or forms, invites a person into the religious life. Again, it is only once one is within that religious life that judgments as to the nature of the divine can best be made. According to **the religious life as artful experience**, then, every individual needs to "lure" himself or herself into the art of the religious life. How does one do this?

---

[25]This is not to imply that the religious life must be reduced to artful experience--only that I find this strategy helpful in presenting the religious life as affectionally intelligible and persuasive. I will return to this issue in the "Conclusion" of this work.

By attending to one's emotional life during the performance of ritual, and by opening oneself up to a broader "education of feeling"--from painters, singers, dancers, actors, and writers. One seeks those who teach what it is to feel. In the realm of theology, few writers have so educated their readers to the feelings inherent in a religious life as Abraham Joshua Heschel. Heschel is a writer who helps "clarify" a person's emotional life. His work bears careful consideration.

CHAPTER 6

ABRAHAM HESCHEL AND THE ART OF WRITING THEOLOGICALLY

The work of Abraham Heschel could have been used extensively in Chapter 5 to articulate the strategy of the religious life as artful experience. Yet Heschel, more than any of the other thinkers mentioned in the previous chapter, is an artist. An in-depth look at his work will reveal the "lure of feeling" of art--including the art of the religious life. Earlier, we saw that William James argued that in the area of religion a person accepts or rejects rational arguments based upon an affective predisposition to reason a certain way. In this chapter we will see that Heschel has the artistic ability to affectively predispose a person to accept **the religious life as artful experience**. Indeed, it was through the work of Heschel that this strategy first suggested itself to me.

Rather than articulating special criteria by which we are to judge the artistic quality of theological writing, our analysis of Heschel's work will be more cogent if we can incorporate the philosophy of art that was already employed in Chapter 5. We want to claim that theology is art in the same way that music or painting is art. To be sure, the content (or "import," as Langer says, FF 52) of different works of art will be different from artist to artist and from medium to medium. Yet we want to be able to say of a theologian that he or she is a great artist in the same way that we can say that a composer or painter is a great artist. If we can do this, we can demonstrate to the cultured despisers of religion that what is at issue is one's choice of art, what one chooses to appropriate from various artists and make one's own.[1] To demonstrate the art of Abraham Heschel, then, we will continue to utilize Susanne Langer's *Feeling And Form* which puts forth, as its subtitle indicates, "A Theory of Art Developed from *Philosophy in a New Key*."

Though her initial discussion of literature in *Feeling and Form* is based on poetry, Langer makes clear that her remarks have broader application: "All forms of literary art, including so-called 'non-fiction' that has artistic value, may be understood by the specialization and extension of poetic devices. All writing illustrates the same creative principles, and the difference between the major literary forms, such as verse and prose, is a difference of devices used in literary creation. . . . The transition to prose literature is very easily made once the principle of poetic creation is understood" (213). Elsewhere she writes: "Prose is a literary use of language, and therefore, in a broad but perfectly legitimate sense (considering the meaning of 'poesis'), a *poetic form*" (FF 257).[2] *A priori* for Langer, therefore, theological writing can be judged on artistic merit.

We can discern from Langer's work three general principles in the art of literary creation. The first is that "the poet's business is to create the appearance of 'experiences,' the semblance of events lived and felt, and to organize them so they constitute a purely and completely experienced reality, a piece of *virtual life*" (FF 212). In creating this virtual life Langer writes that poetry creates "a world of its own" (228). We are immediately struck by this definition of poetry and Santayana's definition of religion ("a world in which to live in"). The possibility for artistic power in theology is evident: literature has the ability of creating the virtual experience of living within a particular

---

[1] It then becomes the task of the religious writer to depict the religious life in an aesthetically powerful and alluring manner.

[2] Langer defines poesis as "the poetic imagination"; she writes that poesis "is a wider term than literature, because there are other modes of poetic imagination than the presentation of life through language alone" (FF 266).

religious world.[3]

As to how literary artists are able to present "a piece of virtual life," we need to go on to Langer's other major assertions about literary creation. She writes of "the principle of poetic creation: virtual events are qualitative in their very constitution--the 'facts' have no existence apart from values; their emotional import is part of their appearance; they cannot, therefore, be stated and then 'reacted to.' They occur only as they seem--they are *poetic facts*, not neutral facts toward which we are invited to take a poetic attitude" (FF 223). The poet thus uses discourse non-discursively. Langer notes that "were poetry essentially a means of stating discursive ideas, whether directly or by implication, it would be more nearly related to metaphysics, logic and mathematics than to any of the arts. But propositions--the basic structures of discourse, which formulate and convey true or false beliefs 'discursively'-- are only materials of poetry" (FF 227). Langer speaks of poetry here the way Eliade speaks of "facts" in religion. Eliade writes of the danger of reducing "spiritual universes . . . to *facts* about social organisations, economic regimes, epochs of precolonial and colonial history, etc." (70). He thus calls for the utilization of "creative hermeneutics" (62) in the history of religions. We might say that accumulated data about religious experience awaits the creative artist to poetically give voice to that experience.

Langer's final "principle of poesis" says that "everything actual must be transformed by imagination into something purely experiential" (FF 258). She identifies the "mnemonic mode" as the imaginative faculty that is key here; and she says that a poetic statement's "purpose is not to inform people of what has happened and when, but to create the illusion of things past, the semblance of events lived and felt, like an abstracted and completed memory" (269). Langer adds that "literature proper is the use of language to create

---

[3]I use "literature" the way I used "art" in the preceding chapter. I refer to literature that *can* express a way of life.

virtual history, or life, in the mnemonic mode--the semblance of memory, into a depersonalized memory. . . . All 'creative writing' is poesis, and so far as it works with words alone, creates the same illusion: virtual memory, or history in the mode of an experienced Past" (274). What this means is that the way a powerful book is affective is akin to the way an individual remembers. The writer has the ability to create virtual experience by depicting those impressions in experience that are recalled by memory. Langer thus writes: "Memory is a special kind of experience, because it is composed of selected impressions, whereas actual experience is a welter of sights, sounds, feelings, physical strains, expectations, and minute, undeveloped reactions" (263). The events of a good novel "become real" the way memory is real--if one were to have a memory of the event of the book they would "read" as the novel does. Similarly, a theologian like Heschel can call forth in the reader's mind what it would be like if one had an experience of being grasped by the ineffable.[4]

Langer, to be sure, does not provide us with a checklist for discerning the artistic value of a work of literature. She does give us insight into what is created in a work of verse or prose. Langer's "virtual experience" and "virtual life" are particularly helpful in speaking about religion. Through religious literature, a writer can allow his or her readers to virtually experience what it feels like to live a life that itself has "virtual dimensions"--a life that has been consciously created and in which "meaning" is not always attached to purpose. Turning to Heschel, then, we will want to examine how he transforms "everything actual into something purely experiential," assembles "poetic facts," and constructs a "piece of virtual life."

In considering the art of Abraham Heschel one scarcely knows where

---

[4]What one does with such a virtual experience of the religious life will concern us later. I shall be arguing that Heschel's presentation of the Jewish religious life does not persuade one to take up the specific ritual demands of that life.

to begin--or end. Heschel is so marvelously lyrical that one is tempted to fill up several pages with his words and let them stand--as art--for themselves. In doing so, however, one would not be any closer to an analysis of *why* Heschel is so powerful and affective. So we must focus on *how* he achieves a powerful virtualism, on his rhetorical range and concern.

Wonder

Who lit the wonder before our eyes and the wonder of our eyes? Who struck the lightning in the minds and scorched us with an imperative of being overawed by the holy as unquenchable as the sight of the stars?

Abraham Heschel, *Man is Not Alone*

I celebrate myself, and sing myself,
And what I assume you shall assume,
For every atom belonging to me as good belongs to you.

I loafe and invite my soul,
I lean and loafe at my ease observing a spear of summer grass.

My tongue, every atom of my blood, form'd from this soil, this air,
Born here of parents born here from parents the same,
and their parents the same,
I, now thirty-seven years old in perfect health begin,
Hoping to cease not till death.

Walt Whitman, "Song of Myself"

A certain type of writing may be called "Whitmanesque," after the nineteenth-century American poet Walt Whitman. It is a style that sings. Whitman exuberantly pronounces himself to the world, and with every "atom" of his being gives voice to the song that is his life. Heschel's writing is Whitmanesque, and *Man is Not Alone* is Heschel's *Leaves of Grass*.[5] Heschel sings of the wonder of the world and the wonder of *being* in the world in a way that leaves no room for equivocation. He does not just say that *he*

---

[5]Significantly, Whitman only wrote one book of poetry, *Leaves of Grass*. Whitman originally published *Leaves of Grass* in 1855, and spent the next thirty years adding (and occasionally subtracting) poems to the book as it went through nine editions (the last, the 1891-1892 edition, appeared just before Whitman died). Whitman dedicated his life to his song.

perceives the world to be full of wonder, but that the world *is* wonder-ful. Whitman similarly makes it clear that *Leaves of Grass* is not just the song of one American man named Walt Whitman. In "Song of Myself," which is to act as an introduction to his life's work, Whitman writes: "In all people I see myself, none more and not one a barley-corn less, / And the good or bad I say of myself I say of them." Whitman is the poet who is one with the American people; Heschel is the writer who is one with humanity.

Consider the above epigraph from *Man is Not Alone* (68). The first sentence is a beautiful example of Heschel's artistry: "Who lit the wonder before our eyes and the wonder of our eyes?" Heschel constantly reminds us that "wonder" is both a noun and a verb, and that *as* a verb it is not only transitive (expressing surprise or curiosity) but intransitive as well: to be filled with wonder. In this sentence only one word in the second clause differentiates it from the first: "Who lit the wonder before our eyes" becomes "Who lit the wonder of our eyes." In this way Heschel is able to link an appreciation for beauty in the world (something which many do appreciate) to that which is only seldom reflected upon: that our awareness of wonder itself bespeaks the ineffable.

The power of the first sentence in this passage carries us through the more wordy second sentence: "Who struck the lightning in the minds and scorched us with an imperative of being overawed by the holy as unquench-able as the sight of the stars?" Heschel continues his use of optical imagery-- depicting "lightning" as striking minds. He then can write of the "scorching," "unquenchable" need of being in awe of the holy; and magnificently he ends the passage back where it began, at a view of the world--in this case, "the sight of the stars." The questions posed by these two sentences are not that hard to answer, for in this passage Heschel has indeed created a "virtual experience" of belief. The artistry here lies not in Heschel's ability to call before our mind's eye images of breathtaking natural beauty, but in his ability to remind us of *the wonder* experienced during those moments. And it was that initial move from "before" to "of" that got us wondering. The recognition that a single word change in a sentence creates a new clause while amplifying and adding to an original clause gives us pause to step back and wonder. Once he has imbued his readers with wonder, Heschel can then utilize this affection for his theological message: that some One did and does light up the world. Heschel is a literary artist and as such he makes use of the tools of his craft--creating the illusion of life by placing one word next to another. In this passage Heschel could have written an engrossing account of a brilliant sunset, but then he simply would have produced an engrossing account of a brilliant sunset--not a passage whose import was wonder-ful. To be sure, it is possible to write an affective depiction of a sunset. Such an account, however, will be affective not because it is able to paint a picture of a sunset, but because the particular assemblage of words in that passage resonates in the emotional life of the reader--so that the sunset (affectively neutral *per se*) is imbued with emotion. Literary artists are concerned more with the experience of an event; journalists profess to be more interested in the event itself (though all reporting participates in hermeneutics). Great artists, therefore, can even convey the experience without an account of the event. Heschel does this here. He transforms the actual event of witnessing natural beauty into the experience of that moment: "Who lit the wonder before our eyes and the wonder of our eyes?"

Wonder and Discursive Thinking

The evidence for the case of **the religious life as artful experience** was presented in the preceding chapter. Here we are exploring how in Heschel "facts" become poetry. Two important things are accomplished if a writer can make the argument for **the religious life as artful experience** through a "lure of feeling." The first is that the reader *feels* that the writer is correct because that "lure of feeling" can predispose the reader to accept the writer's discursive arguments. The second is that the writer creates a paradigm for the reader: just as the writer becomes artist in turning a written text into literary art, so too a person can become artist by transforming a life into a work of art. In the remainder of this chapter we will first concentrate on *Man is Not Alone: A Philosophy of Religion* to locate several passages where facts become poetry. To complete our discussion we move to Heschel's "Philosophy of Judaism," *God in Search of Man*, and briefly look at Heschel's "three starting points of contemplation about God" (GSM 31): the world, the Bible, and the sacred deed.[6]

We already know of Langer's claim that "art is able to articulate feeling in a way that discursive form cannot." Heschel's emphasis on wonder can be seen as part of an argument that maps out the limits of discursive reasoning. In *Man is Not Alone* he writes:

> Religious insights have to be carried over a long distance to reach expression, and they may easily shrivel or even perish on the way from the heart to the lips. Our awareness is immediate, but our interpretations are discursive. They are often casualties of the soul's congested traffic, particularly when under the strain of realizing more than the heart can hear, we compromise with words that carry us away. (MNA 98)

For Heschel, discursive language is always a translation of religious experience; and, as we know from modern literary criticism, all translations are (to some extent) mis-translations. The imagery here is a favorite of Heschel's: referring to the human being as both a physical and a spiritual organism who thus has concomitant physical and spiritual needs. In this passage Heschel tells of "the soul's congested traffic" in a way that speaks of a circulation of the spirit rather than of the blood. In a characteristic twist Heschel points out that what is needed is not soul-searching, for the soul is easily found, but soul-expressing. Nothing is wrong with our souls; it is just

---

[6]Abraham Joshua Heschel, *God In Search of Man: A Philosophy of Judaism* (Philadelphia: Jewish Publication Society, 1955) 31. Henceforth cited as GSM by page alone.

that sometimes we are unable to express what our souls experience. Sometimes our interpretive words "carry us away." In this ending metaphor Heschel plays on a common phrase, to be "carried away," and gives it literal meaning. In the translation from insight to expression we move further and further away from the scene of the original accident of the soul.

Heschel, in fact, asserts that the tension between the soul's awareness of the ineffable and the limitations of discursive interpretations gives rise to the greatest artistic and religious creativity:

> The roots of ultimate insights are found . . . not on the level of discursive thinking, but on the level of wonder and radical amazement, in the depth of awe, in our sensitivity to the mystery, in our awareness of the ineffable. It is the level on which the great things happen to the soul, where the unique insights of art, religion, and philosophy come into being. It is not from experience but *from our inability to experience* what is given to our mind that certainty of the realness of God is derived. (GSM 117)

We come here upon an affective use of italics. Heschel frequently utilizes italics to penetrate to a deeper level of the reader's consciousness (indeed, Heschel indicates that he is writing "*depth-theology*," GSM 7). The italicized phrase, "from our inability to experience" is figuratively and literally stunning. We are well-aware of our inability to *understand* certain things, but do we ever think of our inability to *experience*--especially what is "given to our mind"? If something is given do we not experience it? And if we do not experience it how are we certain of it? Heschel shows us that the certainty of our inability, the certainty of our wonder, our awe, testifies to the ineffable (which he says is "that aspect of reality which by its very nature lies beyond our comprehension, and is acknowledged by the mind to be beyond the scope of the mind," GSM 104). Art and religion, then, arise from this tension between certainty and incompatibility: "The essence of things is ineffable and thus incompatible with the human mind, and it is precisely this *incompatibility* that is the source of all creative thinking in art, religion, and moral living.

We may therefore suggest that just as the discovery of reality's compatibility with the human mind is the root of science, so the discovery of the world's incompatibility with the human mind is the root of artistic and religious insight" (GSM 104). The structure of this last sentence is telling. We recognize in it a characteristic Heschelian turn: compatibility and science are paralleled with incompatibility and artistic and religious insight. The very structure of the sentence (non-discursively) reinforces Heschel's (discursive) argument that wonder rather than certainty is the hallmark of the artist.

In further delineating the role of reason in religion Heschel writes: "Reason is not the measure of all things, not the all-controlling power in the life of man, not the father of all assertions. The cry of a wounded man is not the product of discursive thought. Science cannot be established in terms of art nor art in terms of science. Why, then, should faith depend for its validity upon justification by science?" (MNA 171). The sharp image of a wounded man carries this passage. The "cry," coming at the beginning of the central sentence, poignantly "cries" out to us. One cannot help but stress it in the sentence, and then the truth of the statement is all the more apparent: to cry out is to convey emotion in a way far removed from discursive speech. Earlier, in this same vein, Heschel says that "Man is more than reason. Man is life" (MNA 106; this reminds us of Unamuno's "the end of life is living and not understanding"). For Heschel, the life of a human being can often best be grasped through the non-discursive expressions of art and faith.

There is a mocking tone in Heschel's reference to the cry of a wounded man, for it is obviously not "the product of discursive thought." Heschel uses this tone sparingly; when he does, he is able to turn the tables on the cultured despisers of religion by showing how unreasonable is *their* position. On the previous page in *Man is Not Alone* he thus writes in the same tone: "What does our skepticism desire? To see Him on the television set? To let faith crystallize in hard currency of knowledge?" (170). The notion of seeing God on television points to the limitations of reason in faith. For of course, if God were on television we could not be sure that that was God. God would have to continually prove to us that the image on the television screen was in fact God. But then this is not to have faith: this is to have proof of God. Heschel therefore says: "Reason seeks to integrate the unknown with the known; faith seeks to integrate the unknown with the divine; its ripe fruit is not cold judgment but attachment, action, song and coming close to Him" (171). Making a typical turn at the end of this citation, Heschel switches elements in the sentence--"unknown with the known" becomes "unknown with the divine." In this way Heschel is able to make his point rhetorically: the divine in faith is as the known in reason; both are equally *known*, though the type of knowledge experienced in faith is of the "unknown."

Art and Faith

Heschel speaks of faith as an art. He writes that "the art of awareness of God, the art of sensing His presence in our daily lives cannot be learned off-hand. God's grace resounds in our lives like a staccato. Only by retaining the seemingly disconnected notes comes the ability to grasp the theme" (MNA 88). In this short paragraph Heschel makes use of the art of music to write of the art of faith. The pairing of God's grace with "staccato" is quite apposite. The staccato is a sharp, choppy sound and only when the "disconnected notes" are taken together does one "grasp the theme" of the musical piece. Heschel indicates that God's presence is always with us, but it is only when we can begin to put the moments of religious insight together, only when we can hold together in our hearts the moments when our first child was born, when we first fell in love, when we first allowed ourselves to be touched by another, that we can add the many moments together and get One.

The divine staccato is always present because "God is unwilling to be alone, and man cannot forever remain impervious to what He longs to show. Those of us who cannot keep their striving back find themselves at times within the sight of the unseen and become aglow with its rays. Some of us blush, others wear a mask. Faith is a blush in the presence of God" (MNA 91). Heschel changes his metaphor and speaks of the presence of God as rays of light. The sentence "Faith is a blush in the presence of God" is therefore in keeping with this metaphor, but this sentence is more than metaphoric competence. It is absolutely stunning. Again Heschel is able to fill his readers with wonder. For what is a blush? A blush is a *physical reaction* to a perception. Heschel has taken an image from our ordinary lives and paralleled it with religious experience: To have faith is as natural and normal a reaction as is the physical response to a declaration of love. The spiritual blush is just as ruddy as the physical one. Heschel goes on to say: "It is in our inability to grasp Him that we come closest to him. The existence of God is not real because it is conceivable; it is conceivable because it is real" (91). By now we can see that this last sentence is typical of Heschel's writing. Heschel takes two elements in a clause and turns them around to reveal their true meaning (this is an example of the rhetorical form known as "chiasmus"). After a while one begins to anticipate this rhetoric in Heschel and it thus has all the more affect, for the reader fills in the phrase before it is even read completely. In doing so it is as if the reader has a *virtual memory* of the words and is recalling them in order to complete the sentence. Heschel also plays with the word "inability" (just as he did above with "incompatibility," GSM 104). Were we able to grasp God we would be touching god. He therefore says that

> Authentic faith is more than an echo of a tradition. It is a creative situation, an event. For God is not always silent, and man is not always blind. In every man's life there are moments when there is a lifting of the veil at the horizon of the known, opening a sight of the eternal. Each of us has at least once in his life experienced the momentous reality of God. Each of us has once caught a glimpse

of the beauty, peace and power that flow through the souls of those who are devoted to Him. But such experiences or inspirations are rare events. To some people they are like shooting stars, passing and unremembered. In others they kindle a light that is never quenched. The remembrance of that experience and the loyalty to the response of that moment are the forces that sustain our faith. In this sense, *faith is faithfulness*, loyalty to an event, loyalty to our response. (MNA 165)

To have faith is to creatively, artistically see an experience in one's life as a moment of a "lifting of the veil" (a classic mystical phrase),[7] an event in the life of God as well as in oneself. This paragraph, quoted in its entirety, magnificently displays Heschel's poetry. We see at the beginning of this passage that classic Heschelian turn of a phrase: "For God is not always silent, and man is not always blind (this sentence is repeated verbatim in *God in Search of Man* 138). To convey the virtual experience of these moments of faith Heschel speaks first of "every man's life," and then he moves with weighty repetition to "each of us has at least once," "each of us has once." Heschel shows his faith in the faith of every person. He refuses to believe that people can live their lives without being touched at some point by the ineffable. Heschel's language lovingly invites us into the faith-event--so that we begin to have a virtual memory of what a faith event feels like. We begin to assemble the facts of our spiritual life. The imagery in the passage works wonderfully well. The "veil" of "the horizon" is lifted to reveal the "light of the eternal"; and some "shooting stars" do indeed "kindle a light." At the end of the paragraph we again come upon Heschel's creative use of italics: *faith is faithfulness*. The call, the cry of God is out there; what is needed is the response.

---

[7]Consider this quotation of a Hindu teacher, Swami Vivekananda, in William James' *The Varieties of Religious Experience*: "Every good thought which you think or act upon is simply tearing the veil, as it were, and the purity, the Infinity, the God behind, manifests itself--the eternal Subject of everything, the eternal Witness in this universe, your own Self" (387 n.28).

The Essential Meaning of Religion Lies in Participatory Action

Heschel specifically connects art with artful living when he says in *God in Search of Man*: "Right living is like a work of art, the product of a vision and of a wrestling with concrete situations" (296). In a passage that appears largely verbatim in both *Man is Not Alone* and *God in Search of Man* Heschel writes:

> Religion is more than a creed or an ideology and cannot be understood when detached from acts and events. It comes to light in moments when one's soul is shaken with unmitigated concern about the meaning of all meaning, about one's ultimate commitment which is integrated with one's very existence; in moments when all foregone conclusions, all life-stifling trivialities are suspended; in which the soul is starved for an inkling of eternal reality; in moments of discerning the indestructibly sudden within the perishably constant. (MNA 55-56)[8]

This passage reminds us of Tracy's notion of truth as manifestation. Heschel writes that the truth of religion appears at certain moments during certain events. The beauty of this passage lies in that long second sentence where Heschel sweeps his readers up into the passion of his words. The soul, characteristically for Heschel, takes on visceral reality: the soul is "shaken," the soul is "starved." As Heschel descends deep into the recesses of the human being, the soul comes alive, expressing its needs and desires.[9] One of Heschel's major goals is to awaken this need of the soul in every person. Though he writes that "man is animated by more needs than any other being" (MNA 186), Heschel knows that amidst all these needs the cries of the soul often go unheeded.

Heschel breaks the lengthy second sentence above by using the word

---

[8]In *God in Search of Man* the passage appears on page 7.

[9]This is an instance of "depth-theology." Indeed, a few lines down in this passage as it appears in *God in Search of Man* Heschel explains: "The theme of theology is the content of believing. The theme of the present study is the act of believing. Its purpose is to explore the depth of faith, the substratum out of which belief arises, and its method may be called *depth-theology*" (GSM 7).

"sudden" as a noun. In writing of the "indestructably sudden" we are brought to a "sudden" halt and ponder the usage of this word. Heschel has pulled us off our mooring just as we were in full speed, roaring to the end of the sentence. We have to read the words "indestructibly sudden and the perishably constant" over again and again. When we finally can agree that Heschel does make sense we feel recognition dawn on us. This recognition of ours is precisely a *moment* where a certain truth strikes us. In writing of moments when "one's soul is shaken" Heschel has managed to create a virtual experience of the shaking of a soul. The truth that manifests itself to us, however, is real and not virtual. Heschel has enabled us to feel that there truly are souls and that they can be shaken.

The Presence of God in the World

So far in our discussion of Heschel we have considered several passages (mainly from his "Philosophy of Religion": *Man is Not Alone*) that show off Heschel's artistry, and that can also support **religion as artful experience**. In the remainder of this chapter we will devote most of our attention to Heschel's "Philosophy of Judaism": *God In Search of Man*. In doing so we will add to our portrait of Heschel the artist, and, by using Heschel's own tripartite division of the book, we will also become aware of a critique that needs to be made against him. Heschel writes in *God In Search of Man* that there are "three trails that lead to Him. The first is the way of sensing the presence of God in the world, in things; the second is the way of sensing His presence in the Bible; the third is the way of sensing His presence in sacred deeds" (31). We will see that Heschel's ability to depict God's presence is not equally affective as one moves from world to Bible to deed.

Few writers are able to depict God's presence in the world with such eloquence and grace as Heschel. There are scores of writers who are able to depict the magnificence of the world, but Heschel is able to link this magnificence with the divine. Again the element of wonder is crucial to Heschel in this, for he writes that "mankind will not perish for want of information; but only for want of appreciation. The beginning of our happiness lies in the understanding that life without wonder is not worth living. What we lack is not a will to believe but a will to wonder" (GSM 46). Heschel wants to instill this will to wonder, or rather, Heschel as a religious person cannot help but to write of the world in terms of radical amazement. Heschel thus says: "The profound and perpetual awareness of the wonder of being has become a part of the religious consciousness of the Jew" (48).[10] In contrast, Heschel writes that "life is routine, and routine is resistance to the wonder" (85). It is helpful to recall here that David Tracy argues that "whatever else religion is, it is not boring" (101). Heschel shows how for the religious man and woman life is wonder-fully exciting: one hears all of creation singing of the Creator. *If* life is routine it is wonder-less and boring.

One way of seeing the world with wonder is to view it as a gift. Heschel makes much of the fact that the Bible says that "The Earth is the Lord's" (Lev. 25.23; indeed, this phrase serves as the title for one of his books). "The pious man," says Heschel, "regards the forces of nature, the thoughts of his own mind, life and destiny, as the property of God. Such regard governs his attitude toward all things. He does not grumble when calamities befall him, or lapse into despair; for he knows that all in life is the concern of the divine, because all that is, is in the divine possession" (MNA 291). Viewing the world in this way relieves the human being from trying to constantly manage nature--for there is a divine Proprietor. And so Heschel points out: "In the absolute sense neither the world nor his ["man's"] own life belongs to him. And of the things he does more or less control, he controls

---

[10]To support his point here Heschel cites the "*Modim*" prayer (said thrice daily) that reads in part: "We thank Thee . . . For Thy miracles which are daily with us, For Thy continual marvels . . . " (GSM 48). See *Siddur* 113 for the full text of the prayer.

not the essence but only the appearance, as is evident to anyone who has ever looked with unclouded vision in the face of even a flower or a stone" (MNA 290). We come upon a theme of Heschel's: the fact that today our senses are dull. We are deaf to the call of God, blind to the ineffable in the world, numb to God's touch: "We all wear so much mental make-up, we have almost forfeited our face" (MNA 91). We are unable to really see flowers and stones, unable to experience that these are gifts and not data.

The perception of the wonderful is not given just to the few: "No one is without a sense of awe, a need to adore, an urge to worship. The question only is what to adore, or more specifically, what object is worthy of our supreme worship" (GSM 88). Again we see Heschel's inclusivity. He writes for all people and invites all into the marvels of creation. Just as before he spoke of "each one of us" as participating in sacred moments, here he says that "no one" is without awe; and he adds that "it is hard to live under a sky full of stars and not be struck by its mystery. The sun is endowed with power and beauty, for all eyes to see" (GSM 88). Heschel offers us the complement to the argument mentioned above: those with dulled senses cannot see, but for those who truly look there is wonder.

Heschel draws heavily from Scripture in *God in Search of Man*, and from the traditional liturgy. His technique is to cite a biblical or liturgical passage and then to continually make reference to it so that it almost becomes a mantra. One of these verses is from Isaiah 40.26: "Lift up your eyes on high and see, Who created these?"[11] After citing the verse (99), Heschel refers to it frequently: "*Lift up your eyes on high*. Religion is the

---

[11]Heschel would have known that this comes from the last verse of one of the pivotal *haftorah* (prophetic) readings of the year: *Nachamu* ("Be comforted"). This *haftorah* (Isaiah 40.1-26) is read each year on the Sabbath following the fast-day of *Tish'ah Be-'Av* (which commemorates the destruction of the two Temples), and the comforting message of this last verse gets us back to what Heschel was saying about the world being a gift. Even in their darkest moments Jews can look up at the sky, gaze in wonder, and address the Creator.

result of what man does with his ultimate wonder, with the moments of awe, with the sense of mystery" (111). Here the verse is neither quoted nor written out in full; instead it is inscribed in italics, and its abbreviated form acts as a touchstone for the passage. Religion is a way in which human beings respond to the scandalous provocation of the existence of the universe. Whitehead says that entertainment is what "people do with their freedom" (qtd. in Langer, FF 404). Religion is "what man does with his ultimate wonder." And wonder, adds Heschel, "is the state of our being asked" (GSM 112). The free person can luxuriate in activity that is playful--meaningful without being purposeful. The religious person shapes this play into a response, for "we are asked to wonder, to revere, to think and to live in a way that is compatible with the grandeur and mystery of living" (GSM 112). *Religion comes when a soul is free to wonder.*

It is instructive after our analysis of Kaplan to see what Heschel writes concerning the presence of the divine in the fruits of this earth:

> Let us take a loaf of bread. It is the product of climate, soil and the work of the farmer, merchant and baker. If it were our intention to extol the forces that concurred in producing a loaf of bread, we would have to give praise to the sun and the rain, to the soil and to the intelligence of man. However, it is not these we praise before breaking bread. We say, "Blessed be Thou, O Lord our God, King of the Universe, who brings forth bread from the earth." Empirically speaking, would it not be more correct to give credit to the farmer, the merchant and the baker? To our eyes, it is they who bring forth the bread. Just as we pass over the mystery of vegetation, we go beyond the miracle of cultivation. We bless Him who makes possible both nature and civilization. It is not important to dwell each time on what bread is empirically, namely "an article of food made of the flour of grain, mixed with water, to which yeast is commonly added to produce fermentation, the mixture being kneaded and baked in loaves." It is important to dwell each time on what bread is ultimately. (GSM 63)

Notice that Heschel says that "we go beyond the miracle of cultivation." He is not saying that the fact that the sun, rain, soil, seeds, and human labor act together to produce bread is anything short of miraculous, but he implies that in order to *see* this as a miracle one has to go beyond the cultivation, beyond civilization, to God--who makes possible both nature and civilization. Heschel always pushes a person to the ultimate, to the ineffable, to the divine. The glory that is this world is itself an unstable phenomenon. The human being needs to do something with this glory; it can deify nature, or deify aspects of nature, or see in a loaf of bread, ultimately, God. This is why Heschel writes: "There is neither worship nor ritual without a sense of mystery" (GSM 62). Where for Kaplan the blessing gives one pause to reflect upon the events that led from seed to bread, for Heschel the events themselves become sacred and mysterious as they are subsumed in the God "who brings forth bread from the earth."

The Presence of God in the Bible

The Bible pervades Heschel's entire work. In dealing with the presence of God in the Bible, Heschel discusses the significance that there *is* a Bible, that there *is* revelation. Heschel does not proceed via a close reading of selected passages of the Bible; he conveys what the Bible means ultimately. In typical fashion (utilizing chiasmus and word turns), he writes that "the Bible is God's anthropology rather than man's theology" (GSM 412), that "the Bible is primarily not man's vision of God but God's vision of man" (MNA 129), and that "there are many books about God: the Bible is the book of God" (GSM 247). The human being does not discover God in the Bible. The presence of God in the Bible is secondary to the fact that the human being discovers itself as it exists before God. This is in keeping with the whole theme of Heschel's work here, as expressed in the title of the book *God in Search of Man*. Heschel constantly draws our attention to the fact that there are always two partners in an exchange with the divine: "Revelation was both an event to God and an event to man" (194). Heschel diverts our attention away from the question of where is God, and calls our attention to where is the human being. Revelation is an event for God in that God is finally able to communicate directly to a whole people; it is an event "to man" because a group of human beings were able to remove the stopples that muffle the calls of God. This is why Heschel says that "revelation is not an act of his ["man's"] seeking, but of his being sought after, an act in God's search of man" (GSM 198); and that "it is not God who is an experience of man; it is man who is an experience of God" (GSM 230). All these marvelous chiastic phrases take us out of our discursive thought patterns through their non-discursive rhetorical force. Ostensibly, if one has difficulty with the concept of God participating in human experience, the notion of the human as participating in God's experience should not help matters: if God is a problem, "God's experience" should not be any the less problematic. Yet something wonderful happens when the two phrases come together. The words confound and dumbfound us. The scandal itself of "God who is an experience of man" has always made sense to us. Can we make sense out of "man who is an experience of God"? The possibility that we have been blazing the wrong trail appears before us. What if we have been working on the wrong problem? What if it is not God who is the problem of the human being, but the human being who is God's problem? Can we begin to help God?

Heschel indeed notes that revelation is not a product of discursive reasoning: "Revelation is not an act of interfering with the normal course of natural processes but the act of instilling a new creative moment into the course of history. The chain of causality and of discursive reasoning, in which things and thoughts are fettered, is fixed in the space of endless possibilities like the tongue hanging in a silent bell. It is as if all the universe were fixed to a single point. In revelation the bell rings, and words vibrate through the world" (GSM 211). We all are aware that the mind of the human being is animated by more than discursive reasoning: hopes, fantasies, dreams fill the lives of all people. Heschel points out that it is precisely revelation that gives us cause to imagine a new world--one of "endless possibilities." The metaphor of a "tongue hanging in a silent bell" is particularly appropriate for discursive reasoning--both for what Heschel will do with it in the remainder of the passage (*revelation* causes the bell to ring and words to *vibrate*), and for its ability to shake our expectations. Discursive thought is, surprisingly, depicted as mute--unable to give expression to the yearnings of souls (which are only given the power to speak when called forth by God through revelation). It is also through revelation that God the Creator makes room for the possibility of human creativity. God allows the human being to go beyond the finitude of discursive reasoning, to create worlds that are not structured upon the chain of causality but that nevertheless are filled with human meaning, because God declares that this is good. The art of living comes to be a form of *imitatio Dei*. This is why Heschel says that "ultimately, then, we do not accept the Bible because of reasons, but because if the Bible is a lie all reasons are a fake" (GSM 247). If there is no revelation there is no way of imitating God; there is no way for the human being to transcend its limitations of being the thinking, feeling creature of flesh and blood.

In speaking of the Bible Heschel says that "the Bible is *holiness in words*," and that "it is as if God took these Hebrew words and breathed into them of His power, and the words became a live wire charged with His spirit. To this very day they are hyphens between heaven and earth" (GSM 244). The use of "hyphens" as a description of the words of the Bible is apposite and appealing. Hyphens connect words to words, the Bible connects heaven and earth; and the fact that Heschel uses a literary "connector" strengthens the allusion. Note that Heschel stresses "to this very day." The Bible is given anew each time a person opens it and listens to its words.

In another metaphor Heschel uses a favorite image, drawn from agriculture, to remark upon the fact that the Bible grows perennially. Once planted it springs to life again and again: "The Bible is a seed, God is the sun, but we are the soil. Every generation is expected to bring forth new understanding and new realization" (GSM 274). Elsewhere Heschel writes that "the tree of knowledge grows upon the soil of mystery" (MNA 7), and that "he who plants a tree rises beyond the level of his own intention. He who does a mitsvah plants a tree in the divine garden of eternity" (GSM 316).[12] This imagery is significant because there is an act of faith in the planting of a seed or a bulb. When one comes to plant a tulip bulb in the fall, for example, the idea that this small, hard, gnarled white ball, covered in a brown, crinkly skin, will rise up in the spring to be a lush red tulip with adorning sprigs of green shoots does not seem very reasonable. The bloom of a tulip can make understandable how, given proper cultivation by a people, the seed of God has managed to thrive to this very day.

The Presence of God in Sacred Deeds

In *Man is Not Alone* Heschel writes that "the quest for right living, the question of what is to be done right now, right here, is the authentic core of Jewish religion" (269). In *God in Search of Man*, as we have seen, Heschel speaks of the sacred deed as one of the trails that lead to God. He writes that "this is one of the goals of the Jewish way of living: to experience

---

[12]Another beautiful evocation of this metaphor reads: "Horrified by the discovery of man's power to bring about the annihilation of organic life on this planet, we are today beginning to comprehend that the sense for the sacred is as vital to us as the light of the sun; that the enjoyment of beauty, possessions and safety in civilized society depends upon man's sense for the sacredness of life, upon his reverence for this spark of light in the darkness of selfishness; that once we permit this spark to be quenched, the darkness falls upon us like thunder" (MNA 146). Heschel also uses the metaphor of the coining of money for similar purposes: just as in planting there is an element of faith, the exchange of goods and services for money is predicated upon the faith that the money is valuable. Thus Heschel says that "faith is not a silent treasure to be kept in the seclusion of the soul, but a mint in which to strike the coin of common deeds" (GSM 295); and that human "presence is retained in moments in which *God is not alone*, in which we try to be present in His presence, to let Him enter our daily deeds, in which we coin our thought in the mint of eternity" (GSM 312).

commonplace deeds as spiritual adventures, to feel the hidden love and wisdom in all things" (GSM 49). The artistry of the mitsvot, Judaism's sacred deeds, thus comes to be important for Heschel: a way of bringing religion to life, and life to religion. Like several of the writers mentioned in Chapter 4, Heschel alludes to the art of music in his descriptions of religion: "Spirituality is the goal, not the way of man. In this world music is played on physical instruments, and to the Jew the mitsvot are the instruments on which the holy is carried out. If man were only mind, worship in thought would be the form in which to commune with God. But man is body and soul, and his goal is so to live that both 'his heart and his flesh should sing to the living God'" (GSM 297).[13] Aside from the special non-discursive nature of music, it is also helpful to remember here, as Huizinga indicates, that in some languages the word "play" is used for "the manipulation of musical instruments" (Huizinga 158). And music, according to Huizinga, is especially playful: "Whereas in poetry the words themselves lift the poem, in part at least, out of pure play into the sphere of ideation and judgement, music never leaves the play sphere" (158). The sacred deed allows the Jew to gather up the evanescent notes of ultimate wonder and play them as a melody of life.

Heschel in fact implies that the Jew is called upon not just to play the music of the mitsvot, but to play *with* the music, to interpret it:

> A mitsvah is like a musical score, and its performance is not a mechanical accomplishment but an artistic act. The music in a score is open only to him who has music in his soul. It is not enough to play the notes; one must *be* what he *plays*. It is not

---

[13]Elsewhere, in writing about the mitsvot as art Heschel says: "To those who want to tie their lives to the lasting, the *mitsvot* are an art, pleasing, expressive, full of condensed significance" (GSM 353). Heschel thus writes: "Explanations for the mitsvot are like insights of art criticism; the interpretation can never rival the creative acts of the artist. Reason in the realm of religion is like a whetstone that makes iron sharp, as the saying goes, thought unable itself to cut.... Explanations are translations; they are both useful and inadequate" (GSM 354).

enough to do the mitsvah; one must *live* what he *does*. The goal is to find access to the sacred deed. But the holiness in the mitsvah is only open to him who knows how to discover the holiness in his own soul. . . . With a sacred deed goes a cry of the soul, inarticulate at times, that is more expressive of what we witness, of what we sense than words. (GSM 315-317)

Heschel reminds us that while the performance of the sacred deed is important, the deed does not become music without expression--or, in traditional Jewish terms, without *kavanah* ("attentiveness to God," GSM 315).[14] Heschel can thus say that "the purpose of observance is not to express but to *be* what we feel or think, to unite our existence with that which we feel or think; to be close to the reality that lies beyond all thought and feeling; to be attached to the holy" (GSM 358). He therefore writes that

The task of Jewish philosophy today, is not only to describe the essence but also to set forth the universal relevance of Judaism, the bearings of its demands upon the chance of man to remain human. Bringing to light the lonely splendor of Jewish thinking, conveying the taste of eternity in our daily living is the greatest aid we can render to the man of our time who has fallen so low that he is not even capable of being ashamed of what happened in his days. (GSM 421)

Here, at the end of *God in Search of Man*, Heschel reiterates the importance of discovering the divine in the sacred deed, of "conveying the taste of eternity in our daily living." Yet Heschel speaks *about* the mitsvot--he does not depict or "convey" them to his readers. The rhythms of three daily, fixed prayers are not scrutinized by Heschel, the formative practice of keeping *kashrut* is not touched upon at all, and none of the Jewish holidays is even mentioned in this entire book. Heschel does comment upon Shabbat in *God in Search of Man*, but in a way that does not depart from his book *The Sabbath*--which, as we will see, makes preciously little reference to Shabbat

---

[14]*Kavanah* literally means "intention"; in the context of mitsvot it usually is used to denote the intention of the Jew to fulfill a commandment of God through a ritual act. As I use *kavanah* here, and as Heschel often uses it, its meaning broadens to include the spirited performance of a religious ritual.

life.

What is especially irksome about Heschel's reluctance to mention the particular sacred deeds of the Jew is Heschel's criticism of the way the tradition tends to become rigid. Heschel writes:

> Some people are so occupied collecting shreds and patches of the law, that they hardly think of weaving the pattern of the whole; others are so enchanted by the glamor of generalities, by the image of ideals, that while their eyes fly up, their actions remain below. What we must try to avoid is not only the failure to observe a single mitsvah, but the loss of the whole, the loss of belonging to the spiritual order of Jewish living. The order of Jewish living is meant to be, not a set of rituals but an order of all man's existence, shaping all his traits, interests, and dispositions. . . . (GSM 301)

We can agree with Heschel here: Judaism is a way of living--not a way of being religious, or honest, or healthy. We understand Heschel when he writes: "In their zeal to carry out the ancient injunction, 'make a hedge about the Torah,' many Rabbis failed to heed the warning, 'Do not consider the hedge more important than the vineyard.' Excessive regard for the hedge may spell ruin for the vineyard. The vineyard is being trodded down. It is all but laid waste. Is this the time to insist upon the sanctity of the hedges?" (GSM 302-303). We can also understand his criticism that "the Rabbis established a level of observance which, in modern society, is within the reach of exalted souls but not infrequently beyond the grasp of ordinary men" (GSM 342). But what *is* the level of observance that is within the reach of ordinary people? What is the vineyard of Jewish religious life? How *does* one construct a spiritual order out of one's life? Surely we can hope that Heschel will provide us with a way--at least one way, the way he has chosen of fulfilling the divine command: "You shall keep My laws and My rules, and you shall live by them" (Lev. 18.5).[15]

---

[15]Heschel suggests that this way would incorporate the demands of both halachah and agadah--the Jewish legal and narrative traditions: "Halacha gives us the norms for action; agada, the vision of the ends of living. Halacha prescribes, agada suggests; halacha decrees,

In *The Sabbath*, a book devoted specifically to one aspect of Jewish religious life, we find verbatim the passage in *God in Search of Man* where Heschel writes that the requirements of Rabbinic Law are often "beyond the grasp of ordinary men."[16] Yet Heschel comes no closer to instructing us on the sacred deed here than he did in *God in Search of Man*. In *The Sabbath*, published in 1951, Heschel is more interested in proclaiming "*am yisra'el chai*" ("the people of Israel lives") in the wake of the Holocaust than he is in depicting the Sabbath. In "Eternity Utters a Day," however, we see what Heschel *could* have done. In this seventh chapter of the book he discusses the arrival of Shabbat:

> Then comes the sixth day. Anxiety and tension give place to the excitement that precedes a great event. The Sabbath is still away but the thought of its imminent arrival stirs in the heart a passionate eagerness to be ready and worthy to receive it. . . . When all work is brought to a standstill, the candles are lit. Just as creation began with the word, "Let there be light!" so does the celebration of creation begin with the kindling of lights. (65-66)

Heschel reaches inside himself to depict the affective transformation from *chol* to *kodesh*, from weekday to Shabbat. In the remainder of this chapter Heschel quotes passages from the Friday night liturgy, interspersing between them brief comments of his own. Heschel, for example, ends the chapter with:

> If we only had enough spirit to comprehend His sovereignty, to live in His kingdom. But our mind is weak, divided our spirit.
>
> Spread thou over us thy shelter of peace, direct us aright with Thine good counsel . . . Save us for Thy name's sake. (70)

Heschel reveals the human predicament with his comments; he then cites a liturgical passage to suggest how human need can become prayer. In ending

---

agada inspires; halacha is definite; agada is allusive. . . . Halacha without agada is dead, agada without halacha is wild" (GSM 337).

[16]Abraham Joshua Heschel, *The Sabbath: Its Meaning for Modern Man* (New York: Farrar, Straus and Young, 1951) 17. Henceforth cited by page alone.

with "Save us for Thy name's sake" (a line that marks neither the end of the Friday night liturgy nor the end of a paragraph in that liturgy--see *Siddur* 335), Heschel is able to conclude this chapter with a firm exhortation in the best spirit of Jewish prayer: Jews ask God to save the Jewish people not out of ethnic self-interest, but with the concern--and implied threat--that the integrity of God is intimately connected with the survival of the Jewish people. This is the type of depiction of Shabbat which Heschel is capable of, but which is largely confined to this brief chapter.

In the other parts of *The Sabbath* Heschel mainly writes *about* Shabbat, and he is largely concerned with stressing that "Judaism is a *religion of time* aiming at *the sanctification of time*" (8). Judaism, according to Heschel, thus "seeks to displace the coveting of things in space for *coveting the things in time*, teaching man to covet the seventh day all days of the week" (91). At the end of the book Heschel writes: "A world without time would be a world without God, a world existing in and by itself, without renewal, without a Creator. A world without time would be a world detached from God, a thing in itself, reality without realization. A world in time is a world going on through God; realization of an infinite design; not a thing in itself but a thing for God" (101). There is a veiled warning in this passage: A world without Jews--the people who first sanctified time--is a world without God, without meaning, suffused in chaos. This is Heschel's response to the world that just allowed the Holocaust to occur. It is a courageous, powerful, even comforting response, but in formulating it Heschel does not get at the life of Shabbat. He writes poignantly that "the primary awareness is one of our being *within* the Sabbath rather than of the Sabbath being within us. We may not know whether our understanding is correct, or whether our sentiments are noble, but the air of the day surrounds us like spring which spreads over the land without our aid or notice" (21). But Heschel gives no hint of the difficulty of remaining within the Sabbath amidst a society that does not keep the Sabbath. When is observance a hedge, when a vineyard? To be sure, Heschel had every right to construct *The Sabbath* the way he did. We may be disappointed from an apologetic perspective that more space was not given over to affectional depiction of the Shabbat, but there is no indication by Heschel in *The Sabbath* of a desire to write apologetic theology. In *God in Search of Man*, however, Heschel does state that his book will be devoted in part to discussing the presence of God in the sacred deed. It now remains for us to ask: how successful was Heschel here?

In searching for the divine in the sacred deed Heschel's task was more difficult than it had been in discerning God's presence in the world and in the Bible. Though one can differ as to what constitutes the wonders of the world, and though one can argue about the construction of the biblical canon, Heschel could (and, indeed, did) assume that his readers would accept the facticity of the world and of the Bible--and it would be Heschel's task to show the *ultimate* meaning of their existence. In trying in the twentieth century to discern the presence of God in the sacred deed, however, we would have expected Heschel to articulate some of the deeds that are sacred in Judaism. Yet Heschel assumes that his readers will know what he means by "the sacred deed"; he thus writes about the mitsvot without feeling compelled to identify what is a mitsvah. Jews are no longer living under the hegemony of a rabbinic civilization, however; one aspect of modernity is precisely the disagreement about "the elements of the Jewish way of life." After the rise of Reform, Conservative, Reconstructionist, and Zionist Judaism, to write that "our relation to God cannot be expressed in a belief but rather in the accepting of an order that determines all of life" (GSM 331), is to be obscure about the nature of this order. Of course, Heschel may have wanted to be obscure in depicting the mitsvot. What is a mitsvah to one Jew might be a custom to another, or an embarrassing relic to a third. By speaking *about* the mitsvot rather than depicting them Heschel can include all Jewry--and indeed all people--into his discussion. But to say that Heschel left the order of Jewish living open to his readers' interpretation is to say that Heschel did not adequately blaze that third trail to God: "The way of sensing His presence in sacred deeds" (GSM 31). Heschel gets at the conditions in the human under which sacred words and deeds can be understood. He does not give one a sense for how a particular system of deeds can lead to God. Certainly one cannot pinpoint God's presence in a depiction of the religious life. Yet one can point one's readers to the life of ritual--from where God's presence may be encountered. To do so one needs to write affectively like Heschel, but one also needs to write a rich, detailed account of the religious life.

Heschel preferred to *write about* the art of the sacred deed. This is to say that the art of Abraham Heschel points back upon itself rather than toward the mitsvah. Heschel can thus write *about* the sacred deed:

> Jewish thought is disclosed in Jewish living. This, therefore, is the way of religious existence. We do not explore first and decide afterwards whether to accept the Jewish way of living. We must accept in order to be able to explore. At the beginning is *the commitment, the supreme acquiescence.* . . . By living as Jews we may attain our faith as Jews. We do not have faith because of deeds; we may attain faith through sacred deeds. A Jew is asked to take a *leap of action* rather than a *leap of thought.* He is asked to surpass his needs, to do more than he understands in order to understand more than he does. (GSM 282-283)

We appreciate the beauty of this Heschelian passage, with its use of chiasmus ("explore and accept" becomes "accept and explore"; "more than understands" turns into "understands more"), word plays (not faith *because* but faith *through* deeds), and italicized phrases. This passage, like Heschel's whole discussion of the sacred deed, provides the reader with a virtual experience of religious commitment. Heschel allows the reader to virtually feel what it is to commit oneself to a religious way of life. Heschel, though, does not provide a virtual experience of the specific sacred deeds that actualize religious commitment. While he indicates that there *is* an order, that there *is* a Jewish way of life, the components of this life are not penetrated by his art. Again, we can only guess at Heschel's reluctance here. Perhaps he was aware of the fact that his own traditional conception and practice of the sacred deed was far removed from the lives of his readers. But is there no way of writing of the traditional Jewish way of life--a life which Heschel himself lived--without alienating the non-traditional? Can one write affectively of *kashrut*, for example, to people who do not keep *kashrut?* Can one write of the imperative of abstaining from automotive travel on the Sabbath--even for a worthwhile cause--without imperilling one's voice which also speaks precisely of the need to commit oneself to social causes?

It is a wonderful experience to read a book by Heschel. The artistry of his language is engaging. Heschel is able to create for the reader a virtual experience of what it feels like to be touched by the divine. He is able to create this slice of virtual life primarily through non-discursive means, by writing theological poetry. Skepticism departs as emotion rushes in--emotion controlled by Heschel's narrative. In reading Heschel's work we thus come to be affectively predisposed to the discursive claims Heschel makes: that there is a God, and that God revealed and reveals himself to human beings through the world, the Bible, and the sacred deed. But when one closes a book by Heschel, when the reading is done, what then? What does one do with those feelings implanted by Heschel? These are questions that an apologetic theologian has to ask. Heschel, we recall, wrote that "religious insights" may "perish on the way from the heart to the lips" (MNA 98). Human beings need a way to move from virtual experience to experience. To be sure, "experience" can only *be* virtual within the confines of literature, but sometimes literature can point the way to the art of leading one's life. We needed Heschel to teach us a way. We needed him to take that extra step and delve into the specific grammar of the Jewish religious life through a rich depiction of that life. (Heschel in fact writes that "the goal of Jewish law is to be the grammar of living, dealing with all relations and functions of living," GSM 384.) One senses that for Heschel the religious life was artful experience, we virtually lived and we experienced literary art through his works, but as to how we can now move to making our own lives filled with meaning Heschel is silent.[17]

What we *can* do after reading Heschel is reflect upon the nature of the virtual experience in reading Heschel, and appreciate it as one appreciates all art. Heschel's artistry points most directly to the beauty of artful experience and less to the *religious life* as artful experience. From Heschel we learn more of what it is to be a human being, less of what it means to be a religious Jew. *Unless one already is a religious Jew.* If one is already committed to the religious life, if one knows what the mitsvot are, Heschel can enhance one's life and fill it with beauty. Heschel's affective depiction of God's presence in the world and in the Bible, his remarks upon the art of the mitsvot, and his alluring literary style all come to influence the emotional life of the reader so that he or she comes to be predisposed to accepting **the religious life as artful experience**. Heschel enables the Jew who already *lives* a traditional life to see that the Shabbat, the holidays, *kashrut*, prayers, and even fasts, are spiritual, artistic, playful opportunities. The traditional mitsvot become ways for the Jew to complete God's process of creation by artfully creating a life for himself or herself. And there is *simcha*, there is joy in creation.

One takes away from Heschel, then, a marvelous notion: *the poesis of the religious life*. Heschel writes of the poetry that can become life. This is to say that for Heschel there is always an affective, relational dialogue between the divine, the human, and the world of creation. There is an

---

[17]This was not Heschel's intent. He indicated quite clearly that he wanted to explore how the sacred deed is a way to God, but he failed to do so.

awareness of the divine and all its wonders, and a willingness to respond to the divine. Whether we choose to learn about (or live) a specific *way* of the religious life or not, Heschel has made that life alluring--it sparkles now before us. As Rabbi Tarfon once said (in *Ethics of the Fathers* 2.21): "It is not your duty to finish the work, but neither are you free to desist from it." The wonders of this world are a gift. We did not initiate creation nor will we complete it, but we are utterly unable--"without laying perjury upon our souls"[18]--to refrain from the work of creation, or to still the song that beats in our hearts.

---

[18]This is a wonderful phrase that Heschel uses in both *Man is Not Alone* and in *God in Search of Man*: "No one can be a witness to the nonexistence of God without laying perjury upon his soul" (MNA 81); "He who has ever gone through a moment of radical insight cannot be a witness to God's non-existence without laying perjury upon his soul" (GSM 132-133).

CHAPTER 7
DEPICTION: SHABBAT MORNING

Waking up at 6:30 in the morning does not at first seem to be in keeping with Shabbat. Isn't one supposed to rest? My young children, however, do not yet know about such things as sleeping late. So I must learn from them. My children teach me that Shabbat is not the first half of "weekend." The traditional exhortation of "*koom la-'avodat ha-borei*" ("arise and do the work of thy Creator") still applies on Shabbat. Shabbat is not a day off but a day set apart, a day to be sanctified. Indeed, the Jews of the State of Israel know this very well. Because there is a six-day work week in Israel, Shabbat morning is the only morning when one is regularly able to sleep-in. But what is the common starting time for Shabbat morning services in Israel? 7:30! Why? *Because there is a lot to be done on Shabbat.* This is a deep, deep secret of Shabbat. During the week we strive to make a living; Shabbat reminds us of our *need* to make a self, a community, a world. (Significantly, Jews speak not just of keeping Shabbat, but of "making Shabbes.")[1] On this day one feels the need to study, have festive meals, be intimate (perhaps make love) with one's spouse, play with one's children, go for a walk, visit with neighbors, and yes, take a nap. These activities, most of which one does not have time for during the week, become ethical obligations of Shabbat, part of the *kedushat ha-yom*, the holiness of the day.

---

[1]Pinchas Peli writes that Jews "understood the verse: 'And the children of Israel shall keep the Sabbath... *la'asot et ha-Shabbat*' [Ex. 31.16] to mean that one is not told only to keep the Sabbath, but also to 'make it.'" See his *Shabbat Shalom: A Renewed Encounter With the Sabbath* (Wash., D.C.: B'nai Brith Books, 1988) 96. By consciously "making" a day, Shabbat focuses our attention upon the fact that the human being must make a world for itself. On Shabbat we reflect upon just what kind of world we are creating.

Shabbat teaches us to be just as concerned with one's relations with one's family, just as concerned with one's community, just as concerned with one's physical *sanctification* as one is concerned with one's physical sustenance. *Shabbat is our appointment with ultimate concerns.*

Sometimes on Shabbat morning one wakes to the miracle of cholent. This stew, concocted of meat and marrow bones, beans, onions, garlic, and potatoes (with optional variations including eggs, kasha, barley, chicken, and lamb), takes at least twelve hours to simmer in a crock pot. There is a critical moment in the process when the concoction becomes cholent--which happens well after the food is cooked and edible. My wife and I call this moment "cholentization." The different types of beans become mush and indistinguishable; the mixture congeals somewhat so that the meat and potatoes are embedded in the whole mass. And the smell! One can tell if the stew has "cholentized" simply by the pungent, baked-bean smell of the dish. One goes to bed with an ordinary meat-and-potatoes stew cooking; one rises with the fragrant realization that the angel of cholent has worked its magic again.

But what to eat now, on Shabbat morning? This actually is a sticky halachic (Jewish legal) problem, for ideally one is not supposed to eat at all until the *Kiddush* prayer after morning services.[2] In most congregations outside of Israel, however, services begin between 8:30 and 9:00 and end about 11:30. One is allowed to eat enough, therefore, so that one is not made uncomfortable by hunger during services. The trick is to have a long breakfast without having a big breakfast. For children, Shabbat breakfasts are often the time when they get to be with a parent who normally has to rush off to work during the week. And this morning turns into quality play

---

[2]The reception after services on Saturday morning is itself called "*kiddush*." To alleviate some of the confusion, the *Kiddush* prayer will be capitalized, and the *kiddush* reception will be written in the lower case.

time: the house is fairly dark, there is no radio or television to be put on,[3] the newspaper hasn't even arrived yet; the only thing *to do* is to become absorbed with one's child in a world of play.

Shabbat morning is the Main Event in an Orthodox synagogue. This is the time for the whole community to gather, worship, socialize, and gossip. Everyone makes it his or her business to get to synagogue this morning. This is largely true, though, only of Orthodox synagogues. Attendance on Shabbat morning (provided there is no Bar or Bat Mitzvah) in most non-Orthodox synagogues is, frankly, pathetic. There is no theological reason why this has to be so, but there is a theological explanation for this: only Orthodox Jews feel compelled to go to *shul* on Shabbat. Only Orthodox Jews, by and large, feel that part of what it means for them to be Jewish is to attend synagogue services every Saturday morning. This is the reason why one will often find Jews who do not identify ideologically with the Orthodox (such as myself) attending Orthodox synagogues. As a Reform, Conservative, or Reconstructionist Jew one can obligate oneself on religious grounds to attend services every Saturday morning--but when one gets there it is nice to find a full house rather than empty seats.

Unwavering attendance rather than serious worship is key to Orthodox Shabbat morning services. To be sure, the liturgy is quite important. The actual *Shacharit* (morning) service contains an additional liturgical section (Psalms 19, 34, 90, 91, 135, 136, 33, 92, 93), and other prayers are said specifically marking the *kedushah* (holiness) of Shabbat. Then there is the Torah reading, often a rabbi's sermon, followed by *Musaf* (an "additional service"). Whereas a weekday service (even on Mondays and Thursdays when a small portion of Torah is read) should take no more than forty minutes, the

---

[3]Traditional Jews will not turn electricity on or off on Shabbat. Lights are either left on for all of Shabbat, or are put on timers. Television and radio are deemed too invasive, however, even to be controlled through timers.

Shabbat morning service--including the sermon--takes two and a half hours. But again, while the service has its significance, it is the fact that one can count on seeing one's entire synagogue community during the service that marks the experience of Shabbat morning. One remains in weekly contact with the community. All during the week one makes mental notes to oneself regarding information to exchange on Shabbat: I must ask Dr. C. about my allergies this Shabbat; Can S. babysit for us next week?; Tell R. about my new recipe for potato kugel; Is Mrs. B.'s brother getting better? Of course, one hopes that people will do this weekly catching-up at the *kiddush* following services; although, to the detriment of decorum and respect for the service, sometimes people do not wait. In fact, in many Orthodox synagogues there is a veritable hum--often escalating to a a roar--throughout the service. To be sure, the rabbi will occasionally speak about the halachic prohibition of talking during *davening* (praying), and there is often a decorum committee to keep an eye on people. On the whole, though, the community tolerates what in non-Orthodox synagogues is largely untolerated: the free exercise of one's right to kibitz with one's neighbor. There is more to talk about when one sees a person regularly. This is a paradox of human relations: the more one goes without speaking to a friend, the less there is to talk about with that friend--despite the obvious fact that more has "happened" in the interim. Shabbat morning is a time for people to commune both with God and with each other.

Many of the morning prayers are said unvaryingly every day of the year: weekday, Shabbat, festival, high holiday. This did not have to be the case. The Shabbat liturgy, for example, could have been entirely different from the weekday service. But this is not so: there is continuity from day to day. Shabbat is a taste of eternity; it is not eternity itself. We pray in the grace after meals on Shabbat for a day that is all Shabbat ("*yom she-kulo Shabbat*"), for a messianic age, but we do not live in one. Shabbat time is different from *chol* (weekday) time, but Shabbat is not timeless. Shabbat can be broken--and indeed, it must be broken if there is even the possibility of preventing a loss of life or serious injury. The same "old" prayers (for example, Psalms 145-150) are trotted out and recited. If the sanctity of Shabbat is said to undergird the entire week, here we are reminded that in our pre-messianic age there is a taste of *chol* even in Shabbat.

There is more time for singing on Shabbat. *"El Adon"* (God, the Master"), an alphabetized acrostic prayer sung in most congregations, speaks about God the Creator:

> Good are the luminaries that our God has created,
> He has fashioned them with wisdom, with insight
> and discernment;
> Strength and power has He granted them,
> to be dominant within the world.
> Filled with luster and radiating brightness,
> their luster is beautiful throughout the world;
> Glad as they go forth and exultant as they return,
> they do with awe their Creator's will. (*Siddur* 411)

I prefer the spirited rather than staid melodies that can be used for this piece. Sung energetically, the music strengthens the words of the prayer. The sun, the moon, the stars all joyously do the bidding of God: should we not also?

Unlike the rest of the week, on Shabbat the repetitions of the *Amidah* prayer are for good purpose: to sing.[4] The core of the *Shacharit Amidah* is only four paragraphs long, and all of it can be sung. The melodies of the passages convey the childlike glee with which the Jews receive the Shabbat--just like a small child with a new toy. Indeed, the words of the third paragraph rhetorically speak with childish cadence and simplicity: "And You

---

[4]According to halachah, the purpose of the repetition of the *Amidah*--the central prayer in all traditional Jewish worship services--is to allow even those Jews who do not know Hebrew to fulfill their religious obligation. But today, those Jews who are concerned with halachic obligations are precisely those who know how to pray in Hebrew.

did not give it [the Sabbath] O Lord our God, to the nations of the lands, and You did not make it the inheritance, our King, of the worshipers of graven idols. And in its contentment the uncircumcised shall not abide--for to Israel, Your people, have You given it in love, to the seed of Jacob, whom You have chosen" (*Siddur* 425). Summarized in prose form we could say that Jews here brag that they are chosen. As the prayer is sung, however, one feels more the giddy joy of receiving the day that God calls the "most coveted of days" (*chemdat yamim*).[5] Heschel remarks that "it is as if the command: *Do not covet things of space*, were correlated with the unspoken word: *Do covet things of time*" (*The Sabbath* 91). It is in light of *this* covetousness that the doctrine of chosenness comes to be experienced here. The delight at having a Shabbat is expressed through the concept of chosenness. If the sheer majesty of the universe bespeaks a Creator, the wonderful joy of Shabbat can only point to an "eternal covenant" (Ex. 31.16) between God and a chosen people.

The beginning of the Torah service is marked by much singing. Though we read the verse of "*Va-yehi binso'a ha-'aron*" ("when the Ark would travel": Num. 10.35) any time we take out the Torah, here it is sung. It is preceded by two paragraphs which are also sung, and whose melodies move climactically to the "*Va-yehi binso'a.*" The first paragraph, "*Ein kamocha be-elokim ha-Shem*" (there is none like You among the gods, my Lord") is sung as an overture for what is to come--like two trumpets announcing the arrival of the king. In the second passage, "*Av ha-rachamim*" ("father of compassion"), there is something of a musical interlude. This is a time for reflection and contains a prayer for God to "rebuild the walls of Jerusalem." Musically,

---

[5]In the ArtScroll *Siddur* Rabbi Nosson Scherman, based upon Abudraham notes: "In telling that God completed the labor of Creation, the Torah says '*va-yechal elokim ba-yom ha-shevi'i,*' *on the seventh day God completed* (Gen. 2.2). *Targum Yerushalmi* translates *va-yechal* as *ve-chamid, He coveted;* thus we are told that God coveted the Sabbath, a statement made about no other day" (425).

the "*Av ha-rachamim*" serves to heighten the tension and suspense leading up to the opening of the Ark. The "*Ein kamocha*" served to announce the beginning of the Torah service, the "*Av ha-rachamim*" focuses one's attention directly upon the impending opening of the Ark. Finally, the Ark is opened with a triumphal melody and regal tones. At this moment the verse from Numbers (10.35) comes alive; we sing: "Arise God and let Your foes be scattered, let those who hate You flee from You" from a position of strength. Just as in the time of Moses, it now seems possible that God will help Jews in need today: for isn't that Torah being revealed to us *Torat Mosheh*? The verse from "Moses' Torah" is actualized by the physical presence of the Torah before us so that the moment becomes uncanny and awe-ful. The words of Isaiah that we now sing, "For from Zion the Torah will come forth and the word of God from Jerusalem" (Isaiah 2.3), are born out as the Torah is held by the *chazzan* (cantor). We end this "*Va-yehi binso'a*" paragraph, therefore, with praise for "He who gave the Torah to His people Israel in His holiness." For one singing through these paragraphs, the opening of the Ark is very far removed from Kafka's conception of it as a shooting gallery with dolls without heads.[6] The Torahs seem glorious, magnificent. We are receiving the Torah anew, we are participating in the miracle of revelation.

The passage immediately preceding the taking of the Torah from the Ark, the "*brich sh'may*" ("blessed is the Name"), is in Aramaic. The vast majority of Jews who dutifully read this paragraph could not translate it, but there is something about it that affects one tremendously--especially the last two lines, beginning with "*bay ana rachitz*" ("in Him do I trust"), which are sung. The fact that one does not know the words in a song does not necessarily detract from its affect. Indeed, it can enhance it. One can lose oneself in the life of the melody, in the rich oasis of corporate sound.

---

[6]See Franz Kafka, *Letter to His Father*, trans. Ernst Kaiser and Eithene Wilkins, 1919 (New York: Schocken, 1953) 77.

140

(Catholics who are partial to the Latin Mass might feel the same way about singing in a strange tongue.) The melody of the first half of this song is mournful and poignant; we beseech God to help us in our times of need. In the second half of the song there is a noticeable key change, and we proceed to sing with firm conviction, assured that our prayers will be answered. The overall effect is rather similar to some of the Psalms (cf. Psalm 6) where the speaker begins by recounting the present straits that he or she is in, calls upon God for help, and ends with the conviction that God is *already* helping. When we lift up our voices together, mouthing these strange-sounding Aramaic syllables, joy, happiness, and appreciation are conveyed non-discursively as we receive again that crucial message sung out now by the *chazzan*: "*Sh'ma Yisra'el ha-Shem Elokenu, ha-Shem Echad*" ("Hear, O Israel: The Lord is our God, the Lord is One," Deut. 6.4). Exultantly, as the *chazzan* parades around the synagogue to let the entire congregation kiss the Torah, we cheer in song: "Yours, Lord, are greatness, might, splendor, triumph, and majesty--yes, all that is in heaven and on earth" (1 Chron. 29.11).

Franz Rosenzweig once implied that there are no biblical critics when the Torah is read in synagogue.[7] For the Jew who listens to the Torah in *shul*, the creation of the world *ex nihilo*, angels appearing before Abraham, Isaac, and Jacob, the speaking of Balaam's ass, the splitting of the Red Sea, the giving of the Torah, all are accepted--not as objects of belief--but as facts of the religious experience of the Jewish people. These facts are of a different kind than scientific fact; they more closely resemble poetic facts. They cannot be replicated again and again, but they are nevertheless experienced as true time and again. Heschel pointed out that "the right word is often one that evokes a plurality of meanings and one that must be

---

[7]See Franz Rosenzweig, "The Commandments: Divine or Human," 1924, *On Jewish Learning*, ed. N. N. Glatzer (New York: Schocken, 1965) 122-123.

understood on more than one level. What is a virtue in scientific language is a failure in poetic expression" (GSM 179). In speaking about how the divine has molded the consciousness of a nation, the Torah uses words that are verified not by science but by the lives of the people of Israel.

Belief is not foremost in the minds of those who listen to the Torah in synagogue. The first thing one experiences is the musicianship of the reader: how well does he or she read?[8] Is the voice pleasant, is the tempo right, are all the cantillation ("*trup*") markings being followed? Only after one makes these assessments does one get around to attending to the words, following the story, listening to the Laws, pondering the human frailty and the divine wisdom. Collectively, as we sit there listening to the Torah, we are witness to a practice dating back to the times of Moses and the Kings: the reading of the book of God to the children of God.

In some synagogues the people called up to the Torah ask the sexton to make a special blessing for their respective families. This takes time and in return the person will usually promise a monetary contribution to the synagogue or to a local charity. The longer the blessing, the more money that person should donate. In typical Jewish good humor, after the offering is announced, the rumblings begin: "What! She only gave $50? I gave $100 and she makes twice what I make." "Fifty dollars, huh, I guess the investment banking business is not what it used to be." At these interludes other blessings can be made: for the sick, for the United States of America, for the Israeli Defense Forces, for the birth of a child.

After the final portion of Torah is read the scroll is raised--a process known as *hagbahah*. The Torah is lifted clean-and-jerk fashion (and with an especially heavy Torah the *magbihah* will indeed bask in the exultation of a

---

[8]I realize that in Orthodox synagogues one can only speak of a "he" in reference to the reader, *chazzan*, or rabbi. In my work, though, I want to express the idea that the exclusion of women from public worship roles is fundamentally wrong, and that the pertinent *halachot* need to be reinterpreted.

lift well done), and turned to all sides of the congregation. During this activity the congregation sings: "This is the Torah that Moses placed before the children of Israel [Deut. 4.44], upon the command of God, through Moses' Hand [Num. 9.23]." The present tense of the song underscores the fact that the Torah is one. This, the Torah that we have just now listened to, is the Torah that Jews have always listened to--or rebelled against.

Though congregational chatter often drowns out the *haftorah* reading (from the words of the prophets), this is a beautiful part of the service. The *trup* is different from the Torah cantillation: lighter, calmer, more soothing. It is as if we first have the Law, and then the commentary on the Law to smoothe things out, clear up the unclear. Indeed, the *haftorah* readings usually can be related somehow to the Torah portion. In addition, because the *haftorah* is read from a vocalized text, any person with knowledge of Hebrew and the *trup* can read it without much preparation. The end of the *haftorah* is always sung out in a jubilant manner, followed by several paragraphs of blessings sung in a similar way. The whole Torah service ends as it began: exuberantly, exultantly. When the Torah is now lifted up and carried around the sanctuary *en route* to the Ark, it is almost as if we are part of a champion's entourage, parading around after a victorious performance. Yet our final words are spoken modestly, with the awareness that too often we do not follow the Torah's teachings. We pray to God to open our hearts and minds: "It [the Torah] is a tree of life for those who grasp it, and its supporters are praiseworthy [Prov. 3.18]. Its ways are ways of pleasantness and all its paths are peace [Prov. 3.17]. Bring us back to You God, and we shall return, renew our days as of old [Lam. 5.21]."

In most synagogues the period between the close of the Torah service and the beginning of the *musaf* service is set aside for a sermon. At this point in the morning the attention span of the congregation does not extend beyond twenty minutes and a good rabbi will plan accordingly. A traditional sermon will reflect upon an aspect of the Torah portion of the week. The sermon may often begin with a question concerning the motivation behind a particular character's actions, or it may question the literary significance of a particular Torah phrase, word, or even letter (no letter of the Torah is said to be extraneous or without purpose). The rabbi might then bring in commentators who address the question at hand, offer his or her own explanation, and then point out how the whole issue affects the lives of the congregants today. Given an eloquent, challenging speaker, the sermon can be the high point of the entire service; given a speaker of mediocre ability, the sermon is a time for dozing.[9]

As in *Shacharit*, the repetition of the *Musaf Amidah* is largely sung by the *chazzan* and congregation. The "*Kedushah*" prayer of *Musaf* is often the morning's cantorial highlight. By now all people--even the latecomers--are in *shul* and the "*Kedushah*" provides the *chazzan* with an excellent opportunity to show off his or her voice and to lead the people in song. The "*Kedushah*" is composed of five sections--the fourth stanza being the climax of the prayer. Each section leads into the next. The first section ends with "and the angelic hosts called one to another," the second section begins with that call: "Holy, holy, holy is the Lord of hosts." The second section ends with "the angels proclaim," the third begins with the proclamation: "Praised be the Lord throughout the universe." The third stanza prays for the people who, it concludes, "recite the *Sh'ma*"--and then the people (at the beginning of the fourth stanza) do indeed recite the *Sh'ma*. To emphasize the message of the *Sh'ma* even further, after the words "The Lord is One," all continue to sing: "He is our God; He is our Father; He is our King; He is our Savior; and He will let us hear, in His compassion, for a second time in the presence of all

---

[9]In general, the form of a traditional sermon is the same as any *d'var Torah* (word of Torah). *Divrei Torah* are not restricted to sermons, but are given during life-cycle celebrations and whenever Jews want the words of Scripture to speak to their lives. The following section on Shabbat takes the form of a *d'var Torah*.

the living: 'to be a God to you, I am the Lord Your God'" (Num. 15.41, *Siddur* 465). As Heschel says: "God is not always silent, and man is not always blind" (MNA 164, GSM 138). There will come a time when God will again express care and concern--publicly and decisively--for the Jewish people. There is a tremendous release of tension now with these last climactic words. Musically and rhetorically the "*Kedushah* has been moving to "I am the Lord your God." A particularly gifted *chazzan* will draw the words "*lihiyot la-chem le-Elokim*" ("to be a God to you") out to the full extent of his or her voice--saving every last bit of energy for the final "*le-Elokim*." The moment becomes epiphanic. The rich volume of sound generated by the *chazzan* gives one a taste of what it is like to hear "I am the Lord Your God." Drawing away from this moment, we can only lift our voices, avowing that "God shall live forever--your God, O Zion--from generation to generation, Halleluyah."

The last part of the service begins with the "*Ein ke-Elokenu*" ("There is none like our God"). A young child will usually lead this concluding portion. It is a fairly traumatic experience for the child the first time he or she concludes the service. The child studies with a parent or other teacher and learns how to act as leader for the few concluding songs and prayers. In the child's mind a mistake will be noticed at once. In reality, by this time in the service there is much hubbub in the sanctuary, and few concern themselves too much with a mistake or two. The opening song here, "*Ein ke-Elokenu*," again reflects the childlike playfulness that is found in the liturgy when Jews reflect upon their chosenness: "Who is like our God? Who is like our Lord? Who is like our King? Who is like our Deliverer?" We savor the repetitious wording of this uncomplicated prayer. In Hebrew, the song is even more simplistic as each of the attributes of the divine (God, Lord, King, Deliverer) is preceded by just a single word (in the case of the last stanza, two words): *Ein, Mi, Nodeh, Baruch, Atah Hu* (There is none like, Who is like, Let us give thanks to, Praised be, Thou art). We play with the words. Our lips prance over the recurring syllables like a child hopping over scotched ground. The happy anticipation of the ending of services and the beginning of the ensuing reception further fuels our zeal.

The "*Anim Zemirot*" ("Sweet melodies will I sing to Thee") song is the precise moment of trial for the young person now leading the services. This is his or her moment to shine or sink, for this song is chanted responsively between leader and congregation. How well the child performs will mark not only his or her own stature amongst friends, but point to the child's whole family. Usually, however, the younger the child is (and therefore, the more likely to make a mistake), the cuter he or she is, and the more sympathetic the congregation will be to any flawed performance. Remarkably, though, children as young as five or six manage to do quite well in this solo singing before several hundred people.

Before the concluding hymn of the morning, "*Adon Olam*" ("Master of the Universe"--hearkening back to the theme of God the creator, ruler of the universe, who still rules), there is time for the community bulletin board. Aside from announcing upcoming synagogue events, the *shul* president will also announce congregational *simchas* (literally, "joys"). As the president recites each one (i.e., Mr. and Mrs. Joe and Jane Schwartz announce the engagement of their daughter Dianne), the congregation will cry out "Mazel Tov!"--usually drowning out the next announcement. There is something special about this collective shout of joy. One can feel the full force of community good-will pumped into the two words as they echo from beam to beam of the sanctuary. We are genuinely, unreservedly happy for our neighbor. Deaths, illnesses are not ordinarily announced from the pulpit. There is a time for them too, but here at the conclusion of the Shabbat morning service we shout: "Mazel Tov!"

Most synagogues will make it their business to see to it that there is some refreshment after services--even if there is no special occasion and no sponsor for the *kiddush*. Of course if there is a sponsor, the *kiddush* may be very elaborate, including: kugels, kishka, gefilte fish, cookies, cakes, herring, whiskey, and soda. In some synagogues a *kiddush* may seem more like a meal--and if one forgets oneself it may come to be that. Before partaking of the *kiddush*, the "*Kiddush*" prayer itself is recited, reminding the people that the Sabbath is a "sign forever that in six days God made heaven and earth, and on the seventh day He rested and was refreshed" (Ex. 31.17). Cries of "*L'chayim*" ("To life") then ring out as the *schnapps* begins to flow and people dig into the food--and to each other's lives. "Good Shabbes," "Shabbat Shalom" we say to one and all. Would-be matchmakers go to work, dragging embarrassed single man to embarrassed single woman; others merely gather pertinent information for use at a later date. Children scurry about, running under tables, eating too many sweets for their own good. The adolescents practice the art of flirtation. There is a definite sense in the air here of earned pleasure after the long service. How good it is to drink a "*L'chayim*" and argue about the rabbi's sermon. How good it is to be with people who have been with you every week, through hard times and good times: from the birth of a child to the death of a parent. The social hall resounds with the cacophony of a myriad of conversations, but above the room the sound coheres, circling back down to the congregants, penetrating the soul, bringing with it the sense that our activity here is not merely talk but is part of what it means to build a faithful community of Israel.

The business of socializing taken care of at the *kiddush*, we gather up our children and head home--the morning smell of cholent beckoning.

CHAPTER 8

DEPICTION: A DAY OF REST

For in six days the Lord made heaven and earth, and on the
seventh day He ceased from work and was refreshed.

Exodus 31.17

"*Va-yinafash*," the word that ends the seventeenth verse of the thirty-
first chapter of Exodus, was a source of difficulty for many rabbinic
commentators. "*Va-yinafash*" as it is usually translated--"and was refreshed"--
directly implies that God can be perfected, that God gets tired and needs
refreshment. Two major commentators, Rashi (Solomon ben Isaac: 1040-
1105), and Ramban (Moses ben Nachman: 1194-1270), each consider this
verse and show how it in fact does not ascribe any imperfections to God.
Rashi, maintaining the principle of "the Torah speaks in the language of
human beings" ("*dibrah Torah bilshon b'nai adam*"), claims that God rests on
Shabbat in order to provide a paradigm for human beings: people need a day
of rest in order to refresh themselves.[1] Ramban considers the root of *va-
yinafash* to be *nefesh* (soul). He thus reads *va-yinafash* as "and was given a
soul." According to Ramban, it was through the creation of the Sabbath that
the world was given a spiritual dimension.[2]

---

[1]Rashi underscores the problem posed by this verse by quoting from Isaiah 40.28, which
states that God "never grows faint or weary." The exact language that Rashi uses in
answering this question contains another traditional hermeneutic. He says that all references
to God's "resting" (*menuchah*) in Scripture serve to "penetrate the ear in a way that it can
hear" (*lishbor ha-ozen mah she-hi yecholah lishmo'a*).

[2]Ramban's commentary here is steeped in mysticism. He speaks about the *world* getting
an extra Sabbath soul--"which comes from The Foundation of the world, 'in whose hand is
the soul of every living thing' [Job 12.10]." See Ramban (Nachmanides), *Commentary on the*

How does one rest on Shabbat? How does one utilize the concept of *menuchat Shabbat*, Sabbath rest--whether in Rashi's sense of *imitatio Dei* or in Ramban's sense of an elevated spiritual plane--in a way that sanctifies this day just as powerfully as the rituals of candle-lighting and *Kiddush*?

In reflecting upon the nature of Shabbat, I have come to the conclusion that the *sine qua non* for Shabbat observance in late twentieth-century America is the prohibition regarding the use of motorized vehicles.[3] In order for one to be a *shomer Shabbat*, Sabbath observer, one must be willing to desist from automotive travel for the entire twenty-five hour period from sundown Friday evening to darkness on Saturday night.[4] Every other prohibition on Shabbat is of secondary importance--from cutting to cooking, from writing to carrying. To be sure, I am not saying that transgression of these traditional prohibitions should be encouraged; and I am fully aware of the fact that the rabbis felt so strongly about the prohibition of carrying, for example, that they suspended the blowing of the Shofar (ram's horn) on Rosh Hashana if it fell on the Sabbath lest a person carry the Shofar to synagogue.

Why then this emphasis on abstaining from automotive transportation

---

Torah, trans. Charles B. Chavel, 5 vols. (New York: Shilo, 1973) 2: 548. For a brief discussion of the rabbinic approaches to this verse, see Scherman's note in *Siddur* 337.

[3]According to the halachah (Jewish law), there are 39 main categories of work (*avot mela'chah*), and there are dozens of subcategories (*toledot*)--all of which are prohibited on Shabbat. The rabbis derived the *avot mela'chah* from those activities pertaining to the construction of the Tabernacle. "They based their classification on the fact that the Sabbath commandment was repeated to Moses immediately after the full instructions were given to him for constructing the Tabernacle (Ex. 31.13-17) and again by Moses to the Israelites immediately before he communicated those instructions. It is as if to say that however important, sacred, and urgent the task of building the Tabernacle is--it must not override the duty of refraining from work on the Sabbath" (Peli, *Shabbat Shalom* 34). If one is a halachic Jew, one has no right to single out one of the Sabbath prohibitions (be it an *av mela'chah* or a *toledah*) as crucial while relegating the rest to secondary status--one needs to accept the whole package. In speaking of a "*sine qua non* for Shabbat observance," I am thus on non-halachic ground.

[4]It should be clear that according to the normative reading of the halachah, this prohibition includes travel to synagogue services.

on Shabbat? Because no other prohibition comes close to marking out a community and distinguishing its life as does this one. To begin with, if a Jew cannot drive on Shabbat, he or she must live within walking distance to a synagogue. When one moves into the neighborhood of an Orthodox *shul*, therefore, one automatically moves into a *Jewish neighborhood*, as the majority of members live within a one-mile radius of the synagogue. When one's children go out to play with other kids on the block, chances are a portion of them will be from one's synagogue community. If one takes a Shabbat walk there are many Sabbath-observing homes to visit--and along the way one is likely to meet a fellow congregant. If one is ill or if one is in mourning (sitting *shiv'ah*), one's home will always be crowded with nearby visitors.

Several important philosophers stress in their recent work that meaning only emerges from a community of like thinkers (or believers). Richard Bernstein writes that

> Not only do we need to reexamine the ways in which traditions are vital for understanding scientific development; we must also consider the nature, function, and dynamics of *communities of inquirers*. Pierce claimed that the "very origin of the conception of reality shows that this conception essentially involves the notion of a community, without definite limits, and capable of a definite increase of knowledge." One can make a similar claim about scientific rationality: that it essentially involves the notion of a community.[5]

Meaning--even scientific meaning--comes out of community. The more the members of that community are integrated into each other's lives, the stronger the bonds of that community. One can have a community of scholars, for example, that meets every year without fail at an annual meeting--but then this community only comes to life once a year and is *in*

---

[5]Richard J. Bernstein, *Beyond Objectivism and Relativism: Science, Hermeneutics, and Praxis* (Philadelphia: University of Pennsylvania Press, 1985) 77. Henceforth cited by page alone.

150

potentia for the rest. A real community is *in actu* all the time--whether it is through meeting for daily morning worship services, or through borrowing an egg to bake a cake, or through a simple wave of the hand as one drives past a neighbor. Alasdair MacIntyre says that "what matters at this stage [of civilization] is the construction of local forms of community within which civility and the intellectual and moral life can be sustained."[6] Bernstein quotes this sentence from MacIntyre, and adds that "at a time when the threat of total annihilation no longer seems to be an abstract possibility but the most imminent and real potentiality, it becomes all the more imperative to try to foster and nurture those forms of communal life in which dialogue, conversation, *phronesis* [practical reasoning], practical discourse, and judgment are concretely embodied in our everyday practice" (229). Neither Bernstein nor MacIntyre, however, shows how it is possible to initiate these local communities; in fact, the body of their work here makes the case for why it is so difficult to construct viable communities.[7] Traditional Judaism provides for community through the prohibition of motorized travel on Shabbat.

The establishment of community is a significant result of the prohibition of automotive transportation on Shabbat; however, it is rather a by-product of that prohibition, a fringe benefit, and does not get at the importance of the prohibition itself. Why, for example, after one has moved

---

[6]Alasdair MacIntyre, *After Virtue: A Study in Moral Theory* (Notre Dame: University of Notre Dame Press, 1984) 263.

[7]For MacIntyre, the obstacle to community can be traced to the current moral crises brought on by what he calls "emotivism," which he says is "the doctrine that all evaluative judgments, and more specifically all moral judgments, are *nothing but* expressions of preference, expressions of attitude or feeling, insofar as they are moral or evaluative in character" (12). One cannot *argue* for community in an emotivist world because arguments carry no prescriptive weight--they are merely personal preferences. For Bernstein, the obstacle to community is the struggle to go beyond relativism (which was a reaction to objectivism--hence the title of Bernstein's book: *Beyond Objectivism and Relativism*). Again the question comes up: How does one make an argument for a particular community without negating other communities or relativising away the whole notion of community?

into a Jewish neighborhood, should one abstain from going on an occasional outing on the Sabbath? Why should one not even drive to synagogue on Shabbat? Here we come to the rabbinic concept of *siyyag*, or "fence" around the Law. The prohibition of motorized travel guards ("fences in") the sanctity of Shabbat. It makes it much simpler to tell which activities are *Shabbesdik* and which are not.

The Yiddish word *"Shabbesdik"* may be translated as "Sabbath-like," or better, as "befitting the Sabbath." In the Jewish tradition not only are there activities that are *Shabbesdik*, there are certain attitudes and thoughts that are deemed "befitting the Sabbath." There are no hard and fast rules for what may be considered *Shabbesdik*--this must often be left to an individual's discretion. What for one person is *Shabbesdik*, for another might not be. A professor of Jewish philosophy might feel, for example, that reading a Jewish philosophical work would be too much like what he or she does during *chol* (weekday); another person might regard this activity as one of the most Shabbes-like acts. Yet when we designate the prohibition of automotive transport as essential, we make it clear that all those activities that require motorized travel in order to be accessible are automatically forbidden. Why? What is it in the *kedushah* (sanctity) of Shabbat that is antithetical to motorized transport? *The motorized vehicle both opens the world for a person, and closes one's connection to the past.* Though we live in a world that is radically different from the world of millenia, centuries, or even decades ago, if one subtracts motorized travel from one's existence, the primary means of transportation becomes the same as it has been for the human being throughout time--walking by foot. Walking to synagogue, walking to one's friend on Shabbat, one is put in touch with the centuries of Jews who made similar rounds. The world of the Jewish people is opened as the world of today is put in perspective. With a car (or train, or bus) there is so much to do that one does, ultimately, nothing. One rushes off to a museum, to a concert, to a sale, to a tennis game--there is never enough time for it all. We may think that by ignoring the ban on motorized travel on Shabbat we will be able to visit with more of those whom we care about, but somehow this idea gets lost in its translation. We end up doing more (shopping, touring, cleaning, movies, tennis, concerts)--and being less. Without a car there is, ultimately, everything. There is one's family, one's community, one's Torah, one's God. One is able to hear the commanding voice of all of these; one is able to feel their allure because one is no longer lured to places beyond one's reach.

Lest we forget, the activity of motorized travel itself, especially for the driver, is quite un-*Shabbesdik*. One has to be a *defensive* driver; one has to constantly be on guard lest an accident occur. This feeling of defensiveness continues even when the trip is over, for there is normally a "lag time" between actual experience and affectional perception of an experience: emotions linger on. Also, the machinery of the car makes its own demands: oil, water, tires have to be checked, and engine, transmission, steering, and brake failure *will* occur at some point during one's driving time. Is it worth playing "auto roulette" on Shabbat?

What are Jews in America gaining by turning Shabbat into Saturday? Why do Jews feel the need for two days of Sunday? Herein lies a secret. The reluctance to commit oneself to Shabbat observance often boils down to *a reluctance to give up work on Shabbat*. Though Jews in America by and large no longer have to work on Shabbat, many willingly do so. Many voluntarily give up their Shabbat, their Friday evenings and Saturdays, in order to work--perhaps not every week, perhaps just every month or so--but in doing this the spirit of Shabbat is grievously wounded. One carries one's experience of Shabbat from one Sabbath to the next; one builds upon it. If one works on a Shabbat not only has that specific Shabbat been lost, but many subsequent Sabbaths will be impaired by that work experience. Shabbat can only truly begin to unfold its mysteries to a person who is committed to abstaining from work. If Shabbat is always a potential work day, if one only celebrates Shabbat provided that there is nothing pressing at work, Shabbat becomes Saturday--not an island in time (as Heschel says), but the sixth day of the week.

Funny how it all comes back to the Bible and God's command: "Six days you shall work, but on the seventh day there shall be a Sabbath of complete rest, holy to the Lord" (Ex. 31.15). Those who know the Jewish tradition like to make the (proper) distinction between work and *mela'chah*, thus explaining why carrying a handkerchief, for example, is forbidden on Shabbat while moving a heavy table inside one's house is permissible. Technically, what is prohibited is not "work" but "*mela'chah*" as defined by the 39 *avot mela'chah* and their *toledot*. Some people often have trouble with the concept of "*mela'chah*" since they grow up with the English "work" as defining the basic prohibition on Shabbat. Indeed, the cultured despisers of religion will often pick such an example as the carrying of a handkerchief versus the moving of a table to deride the whole halachic system: surely, they say, the former is less work than the latter. This derision, however, is deceitful, for it presupposes that the prohibition of "work" can be culturally accepted by moderns while that of *mela'chah* is hopelessly antiquated. Yet when all is said and done it is not *mela'chah* that looms as the bar to Shabbat observance, but plain old work. Jews in America violate the Shabbat not because they want to keep open the possibility of *mela'chah* on Shabbat, but because they want to keep open the possibility of work on Shabbat. True, Jews in America *are* committed to a day of rest in the sense of abstention from work *but that day of rest is Sunday*. And they celebrate it the way the vast majority of Americans celebrate Sunday: they sleep late, have brunch, play some ball, watch the game, go to the movies. By emphasizing the prohibition of automotive travel on Shabbat this is brought sharply into focus. Very few of us live within walking distance to work, and even if we do (or work at home), we are often required to travel. A commitment to the Shabbat and the automotive prohibition would entail the commitment to abstaining from work on Shabbat. Surprise of surprises: the problem, the scandal of Shabbat for contemporary Jewry is not that it insufficiently allows for recreation, but that it commands the Jew to desist from work on this day.

Heschel once wrote that "no one is without a sense of awe, a need to adore, an urge to worship. The question only is what to adore, or more specifically, what object is worthy of our supreme worship" (GSM 88). Time and again Heschel would point out that while the human being's instincts are very much in tune with the divine, it often has trouble playing out a melody for living. One can say that the human being is perfectly aware of the need for a day of rest, but has trouble in visualizing what *kind* of day this should be. Shabbat comes into play here; its many rituals and prohibitions serve to articulate a certain type of rest day. If one is to learn from Shabbat, if one is to learn more about what to adore, what to value, what to esteem in this life, then one must begin with the very simple notion that Shabbat is a day of rest--a day when one does not work. In our society the prohibition of motorized vehicles normally excludes the possibility of work. It is the most effective answer to the human question: How to rest?

There is more to Shabbat rest than an examination of prohibitions. But the prohibitions allow us to clear out the clutter from our lives. We "make Shabbes" by means of certain rituals and by abstaining from certain activities deemed to be *chol*. My wife tells a story about how one Friday night when she was a child (growing up in a non-observant home) she asked a close relative to sew a button on a blouse. The woman, a bit perturbed, reminded Sarah that it was Shabbes and that she did not sew on this day. Now at the time this woman worked a full day every Saturday in her grocery store. She perceived this work as necessary for her family's sustenance; but as for the activity of sewing (which is, in fact, prohibited), that was deemed absolutely un-*Shabbesdik* and to be eschewed. This relative was making Shabbes in part through the keeping of the prohibition on sewing. Though this woman regularly violated the prohibition of motorized travel, her action here was courageous. She denied the request of a little girl, whom she loved dearly, because she was upholding the Shabbes. "Making Shabbes" is what the prohibitions are about; they ought not be used as a scorecard for determining whose Shabbat is "better." Let us realize, though, how difficult it is to make Shabbes every single week of the year if one is not committed to the prohibition of automotive travel.

We all want a Shabbat, we all need a Shabbat, but we have to work at it. *Menuchat* Shabbat (Sabbath rest) cannot be turned on and off at various periods during Saturday. The *menuchah* of Shabbat comes from residing within the sanctity of Shabbat. Yes, all the various prohibitions serve to make the Jews a "strange people," and hence are a bulwark against assimilation. But *we need* the prohibitions. During the other six days of the week we pursue what we think we want; Shabbat teaches us what we need. We need to look deeply upon each other's face, we need to take a walk with our family, we need to visit with our neighbors, we need to come together as a community, we need moments of silent devotion and meditation, we need to sing, we need to dance, we need to love. All these are to be *pursued* on Shabbat as we pursued our careers during the week. If we could do all these things and also drive wherever we wanted, watch television, listen to the radio, go shopping, go to the movies, go to the bank, even do a few hours of work--that would be nice. But when do we take time *to do* the things that we instinctively value? We know that we devote our Sundays and weekdays to those other activities. There is little enough time on Shabbat to appreciate all that we have to be thankful for, to sing all that we have to sing, to love all that we have to love. There is already enough to do on Shabbat in nurturing the spark in our souls without igniting a thoroughfare to the world.

PART III

DEPICTING
THE RELIGIOUS LIFE

CHAPTER 9

CONTEMPORARY DEPICTIONS OF THE TRADITIONAL JEWISH LIFE

I have argued that the religious life needs to be affectively depicted if it is to be understood. Having already moved through three depictions of the religious life (Chapters 4, 7, and 8), it is now appropriate to consider the affective aspect of such depictions, and to determine whether a given account of this life presents it as one of anthropological necessity or one of artful experience.[1] Three recent literary presentations of the religious life will be examined in this chapter: "The Dream and How to Live It: Shabbat" by Irving Greenberg (Chapter 5 of his *The Jewish Way: Living the Holidays*); *Shabbat Shalom* by Pinchas Peli; and "Shabbat: An Affectional Depiction" by Theodore Weinberger (Chapters 4, 7, 8, and 10 of this book). All three are roughly the same length, all three concentrate upon Shabbat, and though all three come out of normative, traditional Judaism, all try to make Shabbat alluring--rather than offering a discursive account of the laws concerning Shabbat. By looking at these three texts I attempt to *show* that the two strategies for sustaining religious commitment can be a grammar for analyzing depictions of the religious life. It ought to be possible to discern in a given account of the religious life its persuasive and alluring qualities--as well as its limitations.

Irving Greenberg, "The Dream and How to Live It"

What marks Irving Greenberg's initial presentation of Shabbat is his basic affirmation that on Shabbat all is good: "The world of the Shabbat is

---

[1]These are the criteria outlined in the present work. They need not be taken, though, to be the sole criteria for determining the affectivity of the religious life.

totally different than the weekday universe: There is no work to do, no deprivation. On Shabbat, there is neither anxiety nor bad news."[2] Greenberg adds that "On Shabbat, it is not really that one is forbidden to work, it is that all is perfect, there is nothing to do" (131). One can recognize here a Heschelian move in the clever twist that Greenberg gives to the words of Scripture. Heschel has a way of taking a familiar thought and presenting it in a manner that forces one to think again. Scripture recounts that God said: "Six days you shall labor and do all your work, but the seventh day is a Sabbath of the Lord your God: you shall not work" (Ex. 20.9-10). Says Greenberg: On Shabbat do not do work because there is no work to do. By depicting Shabbat in this way, Greenberg suggests that when one really penetrates into the Shabbat experience one finds it easy to comply with the prohibition on work.

In light of the absence of work on Shabbat there is an emphasis on life itself: one spends "the entire day of Shabbat on being, not doing. It is a proclamation, 'I am, not I do.' If I could do nothing, I would still be me, a person of value" (138). Greenberg here buttresses what he said before about work: since there is no work to be done on Shabbat one simply is--Shabbat thus becomes an affirmation of being. He says further:

> Properly experienced, the Shabbat can be an overflowing source of holiness. Without distraction or outside involvement, one feels other humans becoming present with a vividness and fullness that reveal their image of God. The close family time gives a sense of rootedness and connection that enables the individual to embrace all of life with love. . . . Holiness is not pure projection (which would make it a collective neurosis): it is the discovery of a depth dimension that underlies the material world. (148)

One sees in this passage some characteristic flaws in Greenberg's position. He is inadequate when it comes to expressing feeling, and he uses familiar

---

[2]Irving Greenberg, *The Jewish Way: Living the Holidays* (New York: Summit, 1988) 129. Henceforth cited by page alone.

religious words for little affect. Time and again Greenberg will write about how "one feels" or "one senses," but he does not render the phenomena affectively. Yet I argue that affection most readily emerges through a non-discursive rendering of words. Words like "holiness" and "love" are used here in discursive fashion. These words have become dead metaphors in our language, and if they are to be used affectively they must be incorporated into non-discursive writing. This is why Heschel liberally uses chiasmus and italics, and why he likes such uncommon words as "ineffable": these are techniques through which a text can come alive for the reader.

Consider this sentence which appears later in the chapter, where Greenberg recalls spending Friday summer evenings at a beach house: "As darkness descends one can feel the presence of Shabbat 'thickening' until it is almost palpably real" (167). This is an example of a discursive statement about emotions. Greenberg uses "feel" to try to convey feeling. He does not write with a richness that *evokes* feeling for the reader. Elsewhere he writes that toward the end of Shabbat "one can almost feel the approach of the Redeemer" (174); but again, if one wants to show how it feels to sense the approaching Redeemer one needs to express rather than state feelings. Often a good indicator as to why a passage is unaffecting, why a passage is discursive writing, can be found in the overuse of the forms of the verb "to be." In general, the forms of "be" are some of the least affective verbs. Greenberg uses a lot of them.[3]

One comes to realize that Greenberg divides his chapter on Shabbat, "The Dream and How to Live It," according to its title. Greenberg speaks about Shabbat as "Dream" in the first half of the chapter, while he gets to "How to Live It" in the second half. In the middle of the chapter he

---

[3]Note, for instance, this passage where Greenberg writes about preparations for Shabbat (with forms of the verb "to be" now given added emphasis): "An extra measure of cleanliness *is* created for Shabbat: Rooms *are* straightened, linens *are* changed, showers *are* taken, and fresh clothing *is* donned. . . . Dress *is* also changed totally for Shabbat" (164).

therefore writes: "The language of Jewish faith is primarily action, that is, symbolic statements. . . . What follows is an attempt to describe the actions of Shabbat living and their intended effects" (158). Significantly, this section begins with a list of the 39 traditional categories of work, the *avot mela'chah*. Greenberg writes from an Orthodox perspective, and in any full account of the traditional Shabbat one should be able to find this list. Greenberg includes more detailed description as he recounts the preparations leading to Shabbat:

> The anticipation of Shabbat strengthens from day to day but reaches its peak of intensity on Friday, otherwise known as *erev Shabbat* (the eve of the Sabbath). The house is decorated. The cooking, being done before Shabbat, fills the house with the aroma of food favorites. The table is set especially with the finest silver and china. Every member of the family should take part. . . . Now is the time to slow down the pace deliberately, perhaps listen to music. (164)

While this is a depiction of the onset of Shabbat, it is not a rich depiction. How is the house decorated? What are the food smells? Even though one learns that the table is set with "the finest silver and china," does one get a feel for this? It would have been more helpful here if Greenberg, for example, had written about the special care with which the table is set, or just concentrated upon one detail of the setting--such as the pattern on the china. This is the stuff of virtual memory. In reflecting upon an event certain details will stand out in one's mind, and it is through those details that one gets a sense of the whole.

Greenberg continues with his account of the beginning of Shabbat by writing: "There are countless ways to get into the mood. Each person is unique. Just getting home can be an achievement for some. In Shabbat, as in many other areas, the principle is that 'the reward is commensurate with the effort.' If a particular requirement is a problem, do not give up. Start slowly. Do it in stages. Grow into Shabbat" (165). This passage is important for in it Greenberg turns pointedly to those of his readers who are interested in having more of a Shabbat experience. He is clearly writing apologetically, and he targets those Jews who cannot easily read themselves into his account of the traditional Shabbat.[4] What is troubling about this passage is that instead of writing rich, deep, affectional depiction that could prove alluring, Greenberg finds it necessary to break off his narrative of Shabbat preparation and turn directly to his non-observant Jewish readers. Greenberg interrupts what in his text could possibly influence the affectional predisposition to commit to Shabbat--a rich description of the ritual life. He shows little confidence in his ability of describing ritual life and in having it speak for itself. He either has little trust in the allure of ritual, or he is conscious of his inability to say what needs to be expressed about ritual.

Greenberg's apologetic focus occasionally leads him to cover-up for normative Judaism's sexist (even misogynist) tendencies. He recalls the Mishnah that is recited on Friday evenings (*Bameh Madlikin*, "With what may we light"; *Mishnah Shabbat* Chapter 2), and he says: "Apparently this particular Mishnah text was chosen because it dealt with having fire, light, and heat in the house. Thus, it was a declaration against the view of the Karaites (from the tenth century on) who denied the oral law and allowed no fire in the home on Shabbat. The ultimate purpose of this practice, however, is study. On Shabbat, there is no time pressure, so the Rabbis inserted a study unit in every service" (167). One observes again Greenberg's apologetic strategy of stressing the simplicity of the traditional life ("there is no time pressure" on Shabbat), but in citing this Mishnah Greenberg needed to honestly address one of the harshest patriarchal statements found in all of Jewish liturgy: "For three transgressions women die during childbirth: for

---

[4]Greenberg's earlier remarks about work already hinted at his apologetic interest. In order to make the Shabbat persuasive Greenberg's strategy was to simplify the commandment of "do not do work": if there is no work to be done on Shabbat it is easy not to do work.

being careless regarding [the laws of] menstruation, the tithe from dough, and kindling the [Sabbath] light" (2.6). These lines are a scandal for those who favor the recitation of this Mishnah every Friday night. Why, for example, does the Mishnah not include a list of transgressions for which men die? Though it is possible to deal with these lines without rejecting the traditional observance of Shabbat (one could say, perhaps, that these lines are just meant as exhortation for women to be diligent in the particular commandments for which they are given major responsibility),[5] to bring this Mishnah up and not confront these lines is to present a saccharine version of the tradition.

Greenberg similarly covers up for the tradition's attitude toward women when he writes about the *birkat ha-mazon*, the grace after meals: "When there is a quorum of three people present, a special introductory call to the blessing is added. (If there are ten present, then the call is expanded a bit, adding the name of God. The more people present, then the more God's presence is felt!, 172)." Now, in traditional Judaism, the Judaism that Greenberg writes about, women do not count as "people" in a quorum.[6] Greenberg inexplicably presents traditional Judaism as egalitarian when this is far from the case. Once more, therefore, Greenberg unduly simplifies the demands of the tradition.

When it comes to depicting the particular rituals of Shabbat, the "How to Live It" part of the chapter, Greenberg glosses over specific ritual activity. He does say: "Through repeated acts of sanctification, the flavor of each minute is enhanced. Prayer, kiddush, candle-lighting, learning, eating, dressing, walking, making love--all operate in special ways on this day" (149); and he writes that "in the Shabbat ritual, every gesture--cutting, eating,

---

[5]This is the interpretation given by Scherman in *Siddur* 326-327 n. 6.

[6]There is some rabbinic debate as to whether a group of women can recite the special introduction to the grace after meals. However, if there are both men and women present only the men can be counted toward the quorum, and only a man can lead the grace.

standing or sitting--subtly expresses ideas and values; each movement tells a story through body language and by association" (171). But then when he comes to write about the ritual actions he digresses, gets side-tracked, is incomplete. For example, in writing about the Friday night *Kiddush* Greenberg begins his description by saying: "The family is now ready for kiddush" (169). But this is the first and last statement here on the *Kiddush* that one might characterize as affective depiction. Greenberg goes on to write about the wine of *Kiddush* ("red wine is preferred by Talmudic tradition"); about the recitation of the *Kiddush* ("in some homes, each member of the family has his or her own cup and all recite kiddush, singly or together"); and about the purpose of the *Kiddush* ("the main ritual function of kiddush is to give testimony"). Greenberg does not include in his description any part of the text of the *Kiddush*, nor is he able to convey the experience of it. He cites Heschel, saying that "Kiddush is, in part, an attempt to evoke 'radical amazement' (Heschel) at the beauty of existence" (169), but Greenberg does not seem to realize that in order for a term like "radical amazement" to even be understood by readers, he must affectively express it.

Consider also what Greenberg has to say about the Sabbath *Shacharit* service: "The Shabbat morning services are the most elaborate of the week. The focus shifts from testimony-to-creation to encounter-with-Revelation. The mood is more reflective and intellectual as the initial flush of released emotion is succeeded by calm and awareness of the Eternal" (173). One notices again a failure to include any part of the liturgy under discussion, and a predilection to give a discursive account of moods and emotions rather than an expression of them. More than this, Greenberg does not make himself intelligible. He speaks about having an "encounter-with-Revelation" and an "awareness of the Eternal" as if they are not poetic but scientific facts, as if they are amenable to discursive statements.

166

Greenberg reserves his richest depiction of Shabbat ritual for Havdalah (inexplicably, it is included in the chapter's first section). He delves more deeply into this ritual here than he did in the *Kiddush*. He includes parts of the liturgical text in his account, and he writes more of the experience of the ritual. Yet towards the beginning of his remarks on Havdalah Greenberg says: "Havdalah is one of the liturgical successes of modern Judaism. It is so appealing because of its rich mixture of wine, fragrance, light, and group spirit that many people who do not observe Shabbat still participate in its ceremonies" (154). Now this is patently untrue. It is just about impossible to find Jews who do not observe Shabbat but who yet regularly perform the Havdalah. Indeed, Havdalah is paradigmatic of the ritual crisis today in Judaism. The Havdalah *is* a beautiful, powerful ritual-- but only for those who practice it; and the majority of Jews in America do not practice it. One way of persuading Jews to take up the Havdalah is to write affectional depiction, but Greenberg's prefatory remarks undercut his description. Greenberg again demonstrates little confidence in a description's ability to speak for itself, and so in effect he "loads the dice"--he suggests to his readers that they should do Havdalah because "everyone's doing it."

Unfortunately, even in his description of Havdalah Greenberg does not produce an adequate account of this rite. Consider for example his paragraph about the blessing over the spices:

> The second blessing of Havdalah, over fragrant spices, is really the last blessing of Shabbat. In symbolic language, the last memory of Shabbat should be a fragrant one so the soul will long for its return. The dream is gone, but the fragrance lingers on. The Rabbis stated that on Shabbat there is a symbolic "additional soul." Some commentators explain that the fragrance is for the departing soul, enticing it to come back next Shabbat. Others say the fragrance is meant to sustain the person who feels faint when the sense of loss deepens. (155)

Greenberg dampens the affect of "fragrant" and "fragrance" by using these words five times in rapid succession; he breaks the flow of the passage by needlessly including the clause "in symbolic language" to speak about the memory of Shabbat; and he subdues the magic of the notion of an "additional soul" by labelling it "symbolic." He also (perhaps inadvertently) includes an inner rhyme in the sentence "The dream is gone, but the fragrance lingers on"--making the whole phrase sound trite, almost like a satirical take-off on a perfume ad.

Besides its literary shortcomings, Greenberg's presentation of Shabbat is theologically problematic, since on the one hand he describes a traditional Shabbat, but on the other he allows for non-normative ways of living the tradition. Greenberg thus writes about the non-Orthodox practice of having late Friday-night services:[7] "While it is easy to dismiss the late service, many people have not been able to clear the time for a total Friday night experience. For them, the late service remains a serious expression of involvement in the experience of Shabbat and of the desire to pray with the community" (167). Just what is Greenberg doing here? Earlier he said that there is no work to be done on Shabbat. Here he writes of people who work through the beginning of Shabbat, and can only make time for a late service. Of course, one would not prefer Greenberg to reject these services in hard-line fundamentalist fashion, but one questions why he refers to them at all! It is one thing to refrain from asserting that one has absolute possession of the "right way" of living. It is another to fail to give a cogent account of one's own specific way of life because one has been too busy in accomodating other ways. It seems that Greenberg is reluctant to make a vigorous theological argument. The result is confusion. Here Greenberg shows himself to be aware of the human need to pray and gather as a community, but from what he said earlier it does not seem at all clear how this commu-

---

[7]Aside from the fact that practically all who attend late Friday-night services drive to the synagogue (thus violating halachah), traditional Jews do not attend such services because they often take place after the Friday evening meal (depriving participants of a Shabbat dinner).

nity's expression is powerful and serious.

Confusion is most pronounced at the end of this chapter where Greenberg incorporates into his own text some comments by Rabbi Haskell Bernat, (presumably) a non-Orthodox rabbi. Greenberg does so as a way of helping him to answer the question: "Can there be a Shabbat observance that does not operate by halachic measurements alone yet expresses a coherent commitment to its holiness principle?" (176). With Rabbi Bernat's help, Greenberg writes about "a pluralist approach to Shabbat," one where there is "*a shift in the mode of being*" (177). A passage labelled "*Bernat commentary*" explicates this approach to Shabbat:

> Ideally, this means not working or even doing housework on Shabbat. However, acts of self-expression or in fulfillment of a relationship that would be prohibited by halacha would be affirmed by this criterion. Thus, one might drive to the country to see the trees in bloom but not pick apples from the trees. Calling and traveling to visit with friends or family would be an expression of Shabbat, but shopping would not. Some might accept mowing the lawn or other types of puttering around the house that have recreational effects as a shift of mode of being. Others might object to these activities as manipulative of nature, a tampering with creation. Playing or listening to music would be a valid expression of the fullness of being. The joy of music and art can intensify the pleasure and spiritual depth of Shabbat service and Shabbat rest. (177)

In concluding with "Bernat commentaries" Greenberg appears to be saying that his own experience of Shabbat is not persuasive enough for the vast majority of Jews. Greenberg in effect now says that it takes a good deal of work to gain access to the day on which there is no work: "It takes a conscious, ongoing process of Jewish liberation to undo the assimilated conditioning and develop a proper taste for Jewish modes. To move into this Shabbat mode, therefore, it will take an individual act of will or a major effort at spiritual rebirth or, at the least, seeing life in a fresh pattern" (179-180). But what happened to "The Dream"? What catalyst does Greenberg offer to a person who is not already engaged in this process of spiritual rebirth? Couldn't Greenberg have written as if his life could be persuasive? Greenberg does say in a note that "my personal hope is that once people achieve the level of Shabbat in these formulations they will find themselves closer to the possibility of taking on the halachic Shabbat experience. At the least, however, I believe that these suggestions will bring more of the power of Shabbat into more Jewish homes" (175). But by virtue of what reason does Greenberg have this hope? What are the limitations of Bernat's Shabbat? What possible justification is there for thinking that by sanctioning Bernat's Shabbat there will be an eventual move to a traditional Shabbat? And why even the presumption that a traditional Shabbat should be the goal for Jews?

In allowing for a pluralistic approach to Shabbat Greenberg fails on both counts of the strategies for sustaining religious commitment. He does not articulate a human need that Shabbat effectively fulfills, nor does he make Shabbat alluring. What Greenberg does by way of **religion as anthropological necessity** is to suggest that the Shabbat is an excellent time for leisure and relaxation. What is missing from his account is rhetoric that *shows* why people *need* Shabbat in order to do nothing. As for **the religious life as artful experience**, Greenberg goes half-way: he describes ritual but pulls back from (or fails at) rich depiction. One can now see why Abraham Heschel so avoided an examination of the specific ritual activity of Shabbat. Heschel perhaps feared that by giving a detailed account of "The Jewish Way" (the title of Greenberg's book) he would alienate those who do not live according to this way. Yet Heschel was able to make the reading of Heschel alluring, and he suggested (but did not demonstrate) that the ritual life can be similarly alluring. Greenberg, a much lesser writer than Heschel, gives a limited account of the ritual activity of Shabbat--and then undercuts it by suggesting that these rituals need not be followed scrupulously in order to have a serious experience of Shabbat. Greenberg bows to the Kaplanian harsh realism of a Judaism where people do not follow laws because they are commanded to do so, but he fails to instruct his readers on "How to live it." It is also interesting to remember here that Kaplan, while beginning with the idea of "Judaism without supernaturalism," never considered the ways of the Jews to be nebulous--the civilization of the Jews might change markedly but for Kaplan it certainly existed as an authentic entity. On a descriptive level, therefore, Greenberg fails to present a rich depiction of the religious life of a traditional Jew.

The strength of Greenberg's work lies in his ability to explicate the tradition while consciously allowing a place in his apologetic for those Jews who are not yet ready to assume all the demands of the tradition. One is reminded here of Franz Rosenzweig's division of the Law into "what is doable" and "what is not doable yet."[8] While in no way putting the Jew beyond the demands of the Law (he says that "what is not doable yet must be done nevertheless"), Rosenzweig recognizes that not all of the Law will in fact be practiced--*even by Jews who acknowledge the importance of the Law.* Greenberg's work, then, can be helpful for those Jews who are "not yet" in a position of Orthodox observance.[9] He allows a person along the route of *teshuvah* ("return" to the traditional religious life) to enjoy the fruits of the journey without feeling guilty for the road ahead. The problem, however, with allowing Greenberg to rest in a Rosenzweigian apologetic position is that Greenberg, unlike Rosenzweig, is *not* a Jew who is in a "not yet" situation of observance. Greenberg is an Orthodox Jew--someone who

---

[8] Franz Rosenzweig, "The Builders: Concerning the Law," 1923, *On Jewish Learning,* ed. N. N. Glatzer (New York: Schocken, 1965) 81.

[9] At the end of his chapter on Shabbat, Greenberg specifically refers to this famous Rosenzweigian paradigm of religious observance: "When asked if he [Rosenzweig] observed certain laws (which, in fact, he did not), he would not answer 'no'; he would reply, 'not yet'" (180).

already finds himself observing the great bulk of Jewish Law. One can legitimately expect Greenberg in his apologetic to indicate why the tradition should be observed *today* rather than just validating a person's current religious practices. There is no sense in Greenberg that he has a vital message that he wants to teach, or of an argument that he wants to seriously put forth. One is left with the popular Orthodox idea that the more one observes the better. There is an admission that people need to start somewhere, and so Greenberg calls for pluralism as a way of encompassing all starting points; but there is a failure to understand that people are already "somewhere"--so why should they go anywhere else?

Pinchas Peli, *Shabbat Shalom*

In the preface to his *Shabbat Shalom: A Renewed Encounter With the Sabbath*, Pinchas Peli writes that Abraham Heschel's *The Sabbath* "remains a classic lighthouse to all who wish to truly experience the Sabbath."[10] Later he writes that Heschel was "the thinker who did more than anyone else to enhance the relevance of the Sabbath in modern times . . ." (41). Based upon the analysis of *The Sabbath* already presented, one would have some serious reservations about Peli's broad statements. One would, for example, ask Peli if it is possible to "truly experience" Shabbat without *Kiddush, motsi, birkat ha-mazon,* and Havdalah--rituals that Heschel neglected in *The Sabbath*. The primary purpose of analyzing Peli's work now, however, is to see how he--not Heschel--presents Shabbat. One could surmise that Peli, as devotee of Heschel, will try to write an alluring depiction of Shabbat. This indeed is the case, and in this way Peli goes beyond Greenberg.

Shabbat Shalom contains no chapter numbers; the book is divided into different aspects of Shabbat (similar to the many subheadings that Heschel used to divide the chapters of his books). Peli does not present a chronologi-

---

[10]Pinchas Peli, *Shabbat Shalom: A Renewed Encounter With the Sabbath* (Washington, D.C.: B'nai Brith Books, 1988) xiv. Henceforth cited by page alone.

cal depiction of Shabbat; he weaves around the whole of Shabbat. One might say that the book is divided into the different affections of Shabbat. Peli writes: "The Sabbath was the breath of the spirit of God breathed into the mammoth body of the created world of nature. On the Sabbath, the world of matter obtained a soul" (8).[11] This is an affective statement about Shabbat. Peli sets up the small powerful sentence by the longer one; and significantly, he ends the second sentence with the simple one-syllable word "soul." "Soul" is a common word. Yet what does it really mean to have a soul? The way Peli uses "soul" here, referring in a Heschelian way to the whole world of matter (including inanimate things) as having a soul, gives the reader cause to think and wonder. Peli does not discursively argue his point. By evoking a moment of wonder he *shows* that the world has a soul.

In writing about work on Shabbat Peli says: "It is not that after working for six days, God, or for that matter, humanity, tires and needs rest. The Sabbath was built into the scheme of creation even before the work of creation began. In the words of the liturgist, the Sabbath is 'Last in creation, first in intention,' 'the very purpose of the works of Heaven and Earth'" (19).[12] While Greenberg said that on Shabbat there is no work to do, Peli implies that on Shabbat the ontological existence of work is dwarfed by the presence of Shabbat--a presence that existed before the very idea of work was created. The human being, therefore, is in no position to define the concept of work; work is defined by the pre-existing Shabbat. Peli thus asks: "Is it to be left to the individual to personally decide what is work? Then there would be almost as many varieties of the Sabbath as there are Jews, because what is work for one may be pleasure for another" (34; Peli then goes on to list the

---

[11]One is reminded here of the Ramban's claim that "*va-yinafash*" (Ex. 31.17) indicates that on the Sabbath the world "was given a soul."

[12]Peli's two quotations here are drawn from the Friday night liturgy. The first comes from the "*Lecha Dodi*" prayer, and the second is from the Friday night *Amidah* (see *Siddur* 317, 341).

39 *avot mela'chah*). Here is a radical rejection of the words of Rabbi Bernat. Whereas for Bernat what is work for one Jew might not be work for another (such as the activity of mowing a lawn), Peli emphatically denies that each individual Jew has the right to make this decision. "Work" was defined long ago by God--who set it off against Shabbat.

Peli, in a way reminiscent of Heschel, affirms the absolute integrity of Shabbat. Certain activities are not done on Shabbat because they rupture the very fabric of the created order. Peli writes: "No matter at what financial loss--come Sabbath, all business immediately stops. No buying, no selling--Sabbath is here and no money in the world can equal her value" (45). Peli speaks of the existential integrity of Shabbat in a way that brooks no exceptions. There is no room or place in Peli's text for those people who work a full day every Friday and attend late Friday-night services. Not that Peli is implying that all Jews who do not keep a traditional Shabbat are "bad"; it is just that he does not feel obligated to depict non-traditional expressions of Shabbat. Peli is presenting what he considers to be the authentic Shabbat--variations on the theme would detract from the original composition.

As opposed to Greenberg who suggested a relative ease of abstaining from work on Shabbat (because there is no work to do),[13] Peli writes: "Remembering the Sabbath is more complicated than it sounds. Sometimes it is a valiant feat bordering on the impossible. It is, nonetheless, possible, when a strong will and an unshakable faith are present" (55). Later, Peli asks: "How can you enter into the Sabbath? Isn't it easier said than done?" (91). One sees Peli here trying to temper a Heschelian approach to Shabbat with a Kaplanian one. Shabbat does not make the harsh realities of life

---

[13]Though Greenberg, as indicated above, speaks of the problems of observing Shabbat in an assimilated society, he--unlike Peli--offers no strategy for persuading a person to undertake the *difficult* observance of Shabbat.

disappear; it empowers a person to transcend them for one day a week. Thus Peli writes: "The Sabbath does not 'do away' with sadness and sorrow, it merely requires that all sadness be 'tabled' for one day so that we may not forget that there is also joy and happiness in the world and acquire a more balanced and hopeful picture of life" (57). Peli's whole book is designed to give a person access to this day, entree into *Shabbat kodesh*--the holy Sabbath.

In a section entitled "Sabbath and the Modern Problem of Leisure" Peli points out that people do want a day off--even two--but it does not seem to be Shabbat. In furthering his apologetic ends Peli now utilizes **religion as anthropological necessity.** He will market Shabbat through a Jewish definition of leisure. He does this by developing the two concepts of *mela'chah* and *menuchah*: "The difference between the prohibited *melakhah* and the recommended *menuhah* lies not in the *fact* of creativity, but in the *object* of one's creative powers: whether directed toward oneself or one's environment, the inner world or the outer world. . . . *Menuhah* is, in a sense, religiously enforced leisure" (70). He points out that one of the criteria by which a civilization is measured is through "the quality of its leisure" (71).[14] In fact, Peli cites the Talmud which says that one way a "man's" character is known is through "his" play (*be-sachako*).[15] Peli makes it clear that a hallmark of the Jewish civilization is the way it has elevated leisure through the concept of *menuchah*. One might say here, in Kaplanian fashion, that to belong to the civilization of the Jews is to play as a Jew. And to play as a Jew is to learn the way of *menuchah*, which can be divided into the negative form of *shevitah* ("cessation of activity," 73), and the positive form of *nofesh*.

---

[14]Peli draws here upon the work of Irwin Edman, who was a professor of aesthetics at Columbia University (Peli 71).

[15]The other ways are *be-kiso, be-koso,* and *be-ka'aso*: by a "man's pocket" (how "he" spends money), by the person's "cup" (the use or abuse of alcoholic beverages), and by the person's "temper." The language in the Talmud is exclusivist. See Peli 71.

Peli writes that "*nofesh* does not mean to fulfill yourself but to go outside yourself, to rise beyond yourself; not to discover your identity, but rather to create a new and better identity. . . . *Nofesh* requires of us that we take our creative talents, which during the week are applied to impersonal nature or unengaged society, and turn them inwards to create a new, real self. This is the inner and deeper meaning of *menuhah*. It is re-creation, not relaxation" (75). Here Peli combines the two strategies for sustaining religious commitment. He does more than assert that *menuchah* is the way the Jew plays. He tries to make that *menuchah* alluring by showing how it is re-creation, not relaxation (with the presumption that re-creation is to be preferred to relaxation). His use of the word "*nofesh*" captivates the reader; in pointing out how it is based on the Hebrew for "soul" (*nefesh*), Peli linguistically scores his point: *Menuchah* is "leisure" for the body *and* soul.

Only when Peli comes to discussing Israel and Shabbat do we detect fudging on his part. If Greenberg covered up for the tradition's sexism, Peli covers for Israeli Jews. Peli shows how the word "Shabbat" shares the same root in the Hebrew with the words "returning" or "coming home" (77). Then Peli connects this idea with the Zionist dream of a Jewish state: "The Sabbath undoubtedly had much to do with awakening the Jews for the return to their land in modern times as part of the efforts of the Zionist movement. The abnormality of life in an alien environment, as a minority, even under the best conditions, came to the fore especially on the Sabbath, which set the Jew apart from the majority of the population who marked their day of rest on Friday or Sunday" (79). Peli would have his readers believe that the early Zionists were significantly motivated by a desire to allow Jews to celebrate Shabbat freely. History, however, has shown that the only time when large numbers of Jews immigrated to Israel was when they sought to escape persecution--not to enhance their religious lives. Peli adds this remark about contemporary Israel: "In our day too, it is customary all over Israel for shops, offices and factories to close on Friday at noon, in order to give people some time between affairs of the mundane world and the Sabbath" (101). Now, while it is true that shops close early on Fridays in Israel, it is not so that the populace by and large can celebrate Shabbat properly, but so they can rest up for other, quite un-*Shabbesdik*, Friday night activities.

Though Peli's presentation of modern Israel's observance of Shabbat is not as above-board as one would like, the purpose of his book is to give readers access to Shabbat. Does Peli do this? One sees that Peli is willing to consider the specific rituals of Shabbat, but, like Heschel, he is not interested in evoking the affectional power of them. For example, in considering the *Kiddush* Peli takes up almost a full page of his book to give the entire text of the rite (50), but then he limits his comments to: "Asserting God's creation of the world gives us a certain position vis-a-vis the world. It is a position of mutual acceptance of each other--of humanity and world" (105-106). There is no depiction here of the experience of reciting or of listening to *Kiddush*. Peli (again like Heschel) is much better in reflecting upon the general tone of Shabbat. In a passage laden with chiasmus (a Heschelian favorite technique), Peli writes:

> For the real purpose of life is not to conquer nature, but to conquer the self; not to fashion a city out of a forest, but to fashion a soul out of a human being; not to build bridges, but to build human kindness; not to learn to fly like a bird or swim like a fish, but to walk on the earth like a human being; not to erect skyscrapers, but to establish mercy and justice; not to manufacture an ingenious technical civilization, but to be holy in the midst of unholiness. . . .
> It is the Sabbath that comes to remind us of all this. Six days a week we compete with the natural world--building, subduing, struggling to overcome. On the Sabbath we declare *menuhah* . . . It comes completely independent of us, with the sunset of Friday afternoon, as it did in the very beginning and as it will continually, "a sign forever." (66-67)

This is a poetic passage. Significantly Peli ends here with a brief quotation from Scripture about Shabbat being "a sign forever" (Ex. 31.17). He thus reinforces the concept of Shabbat as an integral part of the divine plan. The first part of this passage does not specifically mention Shabbat, but Peli is able to convey through it the sense that on Shabbat one gets in touch with what is truly important in life. The two opening chiastic phrases reverse expectations. The touchstone words of "self" and "soul" spring out at the reader, calling for a response: what does it mean to conquer a self, to fashion a soul? But Peli overdoes the "not . . . but" construction--so much so that midway in the passage the phrases no longer carry as much rhetorical affect.[16] As the force of the rhetoric weakens, each phrase comes under more careful scrutiny--and some do not stand up well under this examination. Erecting skyscrapers and manufacturing civilizations have no sharp ties with establishing justice and being holy (respectively). One can see that Peli here is obviously writing in the footsteps of Heschel; and though he comes up short artistically, he aims for an affective impact on the reader.

Havdalah, as in Greenberg, is the ritual that gets the most attention in Peli's book. But Peli writes in purely discursive fashion when he describes some of the actions and practices that have grown up around the Havdalah. For instance, he says: "Each one of the acts performed during the *havdalah* ceremony is preceded with a *berakhah*, a blessing announcing the act" (116). Peli does not go on, however, to write of the experience of blessing the wine, or the spices, or the fire.[17] He discusses the significance of each of the objects of the Havdalah, but he does not express what it means to separate

---

[16]The ellipsis here serves to gloss over a section that similarly grows tired: "The real tasks are to learn how to remain civilized in the midst of insanity, how to retain a share of our dignity in the midst of the Dachaus and Buchenwalds, how to keep the mark of Cain from obscuring the image of the divine, how to fashion a home of love and peace, how to create children obedient and reverent, how to find the strength to perform the *mitzvot*, how to bend our will to God's will" (Peli 67).

[17]Peli proceeds to give, in a section quoted elsewhere in this work (200 n.9), a mystical reading to the elements of the Havdalah service.

kodesh from *chol*. Peli saves his non-discursive writing for broad reflections upon Shabbat. In this he goes one step past Heschel--he includes considerations of some of the specific rituals of Shabbat (though he does not make their performance alluring). Presumably, Peli feels that the poetry of his generalizations will influence one to take up the rituals touched upon in the book.

At the end of *Shabbat Shalom*, in a splendid display of affectional writing, Peli exclaims:

> Who knows how many hidden treasures were lost to us because we did not leave ourselves any time free from concern about the past or planning the future? The constant awareness of the non-stop passage of time is one of the things that implants in us existential anxiety and dread of death. Only the Sabbath, the ability to construct an enclave of "special" time, "holy" time, eternal time-within-time, can give us the ability to transcend time with its pressures, its choking *angst* and dread. The Sabbath makes it possible for us to feel for a while "as if all your work is done" and that next week is another beginning, with yet another Sabbath shining at the end of the dark tunnel. If we cannot see it this way, shall we not let our extra soul, the extra dimension of the holy and the "special" within us, see it? Shall we not give it a chance and invite the Sabbath to enter into our lives? (118-119)

Peli plays on the Sabbath as treasure (*"chemdat yamim"*) in the first sentence. The opening is a call that most moderns can readily accept: there *is* little unpressurized time. Like Greenberg, Peli shows his awareness of the need for "free" time, and will claim that Shabbat answers this need. But Peli moves beyond Greenberg by showing that the way Shabbat meets this need is to *free* time, to transcend time through a day that is given over to *kedushah*. Peli ends the book in a way that Heschel might have. Heschel was fond of reversing what one takes to be questions and what one takes to be answers. Heschel, for example, writes that *"religion begins with God's question and man's answer"* (MNA 76). Peli in effect says that the Sabbath is a question posed to the soul of the human being. Since Shabbat is built into creation and comes inexorably every Friday evening, the only thing for a person to decide is whether he or she will listen to the call of Shabbat. Significantly, Peli ends his own work with a question. The reader is affectively invited to listen to the question of Shabbat, and to the answer of the soul.

One sees, therefore, that Peli manages to combine some of the features stressed in both **religion as anthropological necessity** and **religion as artful experience**--though his poetry is not as magnificent as Heschel's and his toughness is not as hardheaded as Kaplan's. Peli claims that Shabbat is easier said than done, but does not feel that there needs to be significant changes in the traditional Shabbat. While he is entitled to make this claim, a more ample depiction of the life of Shabbat would have been in order--to show how it is possible to experience a *menuchat Shabbat* (restful Sabbath) without getting bogged down in worrying about all the myriad of proscribed *mela'chot* of Shabbat. From an apologetic perspective, Peli's use of **the religious life as artful experience** is more effective than Heschel's since Peli points more directly to the experience that has the potential of becoming art. Closing *Shabbat Shalom*, however, one is left thirsting to learn more about how a traditional Shabbat is actually lived.

Theodore Weinberger, "Shabbat: An Affectional Depiction"

What distinguishes my account of Shabbat from these others is my focus on the life of ritual--especially that of the liturgy. When writers like Peli and Greenberg cite liturgical texts they do so either to provide information as to what is actually being said in a particular service, or they use them as reservoirs for theological statements. I prefer to exposit the experience of the liturgy. I describe what it means for a person to utter certain words at certain times during certain rituals. In this way I seek not only to make the reading of my text an affective experience, but I try to make the religious life itself alluring. It will also be seen that I explore how the work of the religious anthropologists can inform one's understanding of the performance of ritual. Remember that Susanne Langer said that "a rite regularly performed is . . . a disciplined rehearsal of 'right attitudes'" (PNK 134). I am interested not only in the "right attitudes" that a ritual expresses, but in how that rite comes to be regularly performed.

My method of evoking the liturgical experience for the reader is to concentrate on those texts that are accompanied by particularly affecting music. I hope to effectively and affectively create a virtual experience of the liturgy. My depiction of the start of the Torah service (138-139), for example, considers what it means to receive the Torah. I show how the music underscores the dramatic proceedings leading up to the "*Sh'ma*" proclamation. I save my major depictions of the liturgical experience for the last chapter of the book, "*Minchah, Shalesheedis, Havdalah.*" There I focus closely upon songs sung during the latter part of Shabbat to show how music and text affectively express the emotional state of the Jew. I pay special attention to my depiction of the singing of the twenty-third psalm at *Shalesheedis* (the third meal of Shabbat). The account begins in the third person singular, but even then I let the text meld into the text of the psalms: "The first part [of the psalm] has a pleading quality, more beseeching God than affirming that 'The Lord is my shepherd; I lack nothing . . .'" (194). Right from the beginning of my depiction I invite the reader not only into my text but into the text of the psalm. Because of this, my move into the first person plural midway in the description is graceful: "This new-found strength is needed here as we approach the darkest words of the psalm" (194). The reader and I descend together with the melodic line to the "valley of deepest darkness" (Psalm 23.4). When I write at the end of the depiction, therefore, that the wordless singing at the close of the psalm "playfully rehears[es] the soulful passage recounted in the song" (195), the reader may realize that he or she too has just been guided along an affective journey.

At the end of Chapter 7 one comes upon another section where I shift perspective in my writing to draw the reader into the narrative. I weave in and out of my account of Shabbat: occasionally I am observer, occasionally witness, occasionally participant. I begin this section by observing the "sense in the air" of the synagogue social hall; then I move to an immediate perception: "How good it is to drink a *'L'chayim'*"; and then I again step back: "The social hall resounds with the cacophony of a myriad of conversations" (146). These shifting perspectives are affective in that they provide the reader with a virtual memory of the *kiddush* reception. Memory, one recalls, is not readily translatable into discursive narrative. Memories do not usually come neatly wrapped with a beginning, middle, and an end. I wish to convey to the reader not just a description of the *kiddush*, but a *sense* of the *kiddush*. My method of doing so is through shifting narrative perspectives.

One more instance of this kind of writing comes at the beginning of Chapter 4 where I write about candle-lighting:

> Finally sundown arrives and the woman of the house lights the Shabbat candles. For children, there is something magical about watching their mother usher in the Shabbat. I remember my mother waving her hands before she quietly recited the blessing over the candles. It always seemed as if she was physically welcoming in the Shabbat with her hands--before the roll of the hands, weekday; afterwards: "Good Shabbes" says Mom as she kisses each one of us. This is what the beginning of Shabbat is about: making the transition from *chol* to *kodesh* . . . . (67)

By shifting repeatedly from third person to first person in the narrative I am able to make intelligible what it feels like to watch one's mother light Shabbat candles. I make an observation about the practice of candle-lighting; then I remember back to my own mother lighting candles; then I go a further step and am an immediate witness to the candle-lighting ceremony; and then I withdraw and make another observation. I tease and play with the reader. The reader gets small glimpses of what it means to have a Shabbat. But the reader is never allowed to feel as if he or she is vicariously *experiencing*

Shabbat. I keep in mind the twin goals of making my own writing alluring and making Shabbat alluring. I am well aware of the fact that whatever I write it will still be writing and the person who reads it will be reading--not observing Shabbat.

A problem with emphasizing the musical accompaniment to the liturgy is that this seems to make the general claim that in order for a liturgical text to be affective it has to be sung. I give no indication, for example, of the power of the main component of every traditional Jewish prayer service, the *Amidah*, which after all is prayed in silence. The reader will be tempted to question how much the words of the texts matter to me--whether the words merely act as background sitmuli for the musical experience. But here one comes to the heart of my work. The way I know of making the liturgy understandable and alluring is through music. Theologically I am close to Kaplan; tactically I am close to Heschel. That is, when I say, "the more congregational singing there is in a service, the more vital it is" (68), I am using music (rather than God) to provide a rationale for worship. I am able to speak of prayer without supernaturalism because it is rational to wish to engage in deep, affectional experience (which is provided by the music of the prayers). The way I have of offering a rational *backing* to my statement on music here, however, is to write like Heschel not Kaplan. I must demonstrate that the ritual experience *can* be affecting. So I write like Heschel but go where Heschel did not go--deep into the experience of the religious life. I produce a text that is not only appealing in itself but points to the appeal of the religious life.

In my description of Havdalah, a rite that Greenberg and Peli each considered in detail, I demonstrate rich, affective writing. In my opening account of the ritual one sees again an interplay between liturgical text, musical accompaniment, and ritual experience. Since Greenberg was criticized for his account of the blessing over the spices, it will be most useful to turn directly to my depiction of this blessing. I begin the narrative by discussing the materials of this part of the Havdalah: the *besamim* (spices) themselves and their containers. When I first mention those spices most commonly used I simply say "cinnamon and cloves." Then, when I move on to describing the *besamim* boxes I write: "Traditional *besamim* boxes remind one of palacial towers, and contain a small door which when opened reveals a treasure trove of fragrant cloves and cinnamon sticks" (201). By adding to the description of "cinnamon and cloves" I artfully round out the metaphor of the sentence: the boxes look like towers, they are said to hold a "treasure trove," and the description of the spices is then suitably embellished. The reader virtually experiences what it feels like to open a spice box and be comforted.

I do not mention the familiar notion of the *besamim* coming to soothe a person over the loss of the *neshamah yeterah*, the extra Sabbath soul. Though this concept appears later in my depiction of Havdalah,[18] here I am interested in conveying the sense of being comforted--and even more: the sense of the wonder of being comforted. To do this, I bring my son Nathan into the description of the blessing, and describe his reaction to the *besamim* (201). I draw upon both the instinctive wonder of an infant confronted with a new object, and upon my own wonder at witnessing the growth and life of my son, to catch for a fleeting moment what it means to breathe in the smell of cinnamon and cloves and experience it as balm for an abandoned soul. I do not dwell on this moment, however; and through a humorous comment

---

[18]Almost all accounts of Havdalah will mention the *neshamah yeterah* in connection with the *besamim*, but this only discursively describes what is supposed to happen to a person at this time. I prefer to mention the *neshamah yeterah* in connection with the blessing over the fire: "There is an eerie quality to holding this torch aloft inside our home. The flames seem to be struggling to ascend to the heavens, imitating the departing *neshamah yeterah*" (202). Here I use the concept of the extra soul for full affective power. Though the flames of the fire are typically described as elucidating the distinction between "light and dark" (words from the text of the service), in linking the flames with the *neshamah yeterah* I dramatically display that "eerie" Havdalah sense to the reader.

I immediately draw the reader away from this spot of quiet transcendence.

Significantly, I use the end of the *besamim* experience for the start of the blessing over the fire (201). I make it perfectly clear that the *besamim* experience is embedded in the whole Havdalah rite (just as I argue that Havdalah is an expression of one's whole experience of Shabbat). The *besamim* blessing is grounded in Havdalah which is grounded in Shabbat. I argue implicitly for what I had earlier made explicit: that the Shabbat experience is more intelligible and more affecting when it is presented whole. I thus corroborate in my depiction of the various periods of Shabbat Mary Douglas' claim that "events which come in regular sequence acquire a meaning from relation with others in the sequence" (Douglas 65). Rhetorically I *show* that, for example, the blessing over the fire at Havdalah acquires meaning through the blessing over the spices that precedes it.

The reader will recognize in my writing some techniques used by Heschel. I occasionally highlight a particular phrase in italics, I end sections of my work with questions calling for responses, and I pay close attention to metaphors. Consider the concluding sentence to Chapter 8: "There is already enough to do on Shabbat in nurturing the spark in our souls without igniting a thoroughfare to the world" (155). The sentence obviously revolves around the complementary words "spark" and "igniting." But notice how "igniting a thoroughfare to the world" contrasts with "nurturing the spark in our souls." A comforting, soothing word, "nurturing," is set off against the harsh "igniting" so that the latter clause is found unattractive. Because of the metaphoric linkage I can end my sentence by speaking about a "thoroughfare to the world," and one realizes that the whole chapter has come together. I have, at the end of a chapter in which I stress the importance of abstaining from automotive travel on the Sabbath, poetically strengthened my argument.

At the beginning of that last sentence of Chapter 8 I speak about there being "enough to do on Shabbat." This idea serves as my major rational justification for Shabbat observance, and through it I make effective use of **religion as anthropological necessity**. Greenberg, one remembers, had argued that there is nothing to do on Shabbat. He perceived the need of American Jews for a day off and presented the Shabbat as such a day. I look about me at the hustle and bustle of American Jews on Saturday and offer them a day that is also full of activity--but activity of a different sort than Saturday. Whereas Greenberg had said that one spends the "Shabbat on being, not doing" (Greenberg 138), I improvise on this concept. I write that in the process of turning Shabbat into Saturday "we end up doing more . . . and being less" (152). I draw the reader's attention to the fact that there are certain activities that are more conducive to being than others, and that traditional Shabbat observance emphasizes things to do that involve *being* more. I thus write: "During the other six days of the week we pursue what we think we want; Shabbat teaches us what we need" (155).[19] On the one hand I point out, in addressing those people who feel that they need to do things on Saturday, that there is much to do on Shabbat and that it is a question of choosing what to do (a choice for Shabbat standing as a choice for doing things that enhance being). On the other hand, I imply that the human being needs to give itself over to the Shabbat because it does not really know what it needs. In a way I acknowledge in my text that even if presented with the Shabbat as "doing" things, American Jews might not opt for Shabbat. There is a call here for that Heschelian leap of action (see GSM 283). But I narrow the span of the leap by richly depicting the ritual life. My approach to **religion as anthropological necessity**, therefore, is more adequate than Greenberg's because it takes into account a demonstrable need of American Jews, the need to do things on Saturday, and seeks to channel this need into the doing of the things of Shabbat. Greenberg *posits*

---

[19]I also say: "People might think that they want to go partying every Friday night, but Shabbat tells them that they are tired, that they need a good night's sleep" (74).

the need for a traditional Shabbat, but does not show how the lives of American Jews bespeak this need.

I repeatedly play on this concept of "doing" on Shabbat. In the penultimate sentence of Chapter 4 I write: "See, there is nothing *to do* on Shabbat--no television, movies, bars, concerts, ballet" (75). Yet in the final sentence to the chapter one realizes that I was *satirizing* all those who claim that there is nothing to do on Shabbat--because I intimate that "there are things worthwhile that do not involve those activities"--"things" that I describe in the chapter and continue to develop. That I was satirizing the cultured despisers of religion at the end of Chapter 4 can readily be seen at the beginning of Chapter 7 where I write that "*there is a lot to be done on Shabbat,*" and that "*Shabbat is our appointment with ultimate concerns*" (133, 134). In a way reminiscent of Heschel, these statements are italicized in my text and spring out at the reader. Notice too my use of "appointment" and "concerns" (with their businesslike connotations) to describe the activity of Shabbat--thus reinforcing the idea that there is important activity to be done on this day. And the notion of there being a lot to do on Shabbat, though I use it as a strategy of religion as anthropologcial necessity, is itself very Heschelian. Every one knows that the Sabbath is a day of rest. If one speaks about Shabbat as a day on which there is much to do, that serves to bring the reader up short, and makes the reader take notice of what is being said. In speaking about the close of Shabbat, therefore, I write: "Shabbat does not end with darkness--it ends with *Havdalah*" (195). Taken out of context this sentence seems to be nit-picking, for darkness *is* linked with the end of Shabbat (one can only recite Havdalah on Saturday night when it is dark). But this is precisely the point: most readers would expect me, in leading into the account of Havdalah to write something like: "As darkness descends it is time for Havdalah." I reverse the reader's expectation here in a way that Heschel so often did. In doing so I challenge the reader to carefully attend to my writing, to find out what I mean by making the surprising claims that there is a lot to do on Shabbat and that darkness does not end Shabbat.[20]

I deepen my use of this reversal-of-expectations technique in my discussion in Chapter 8 of *mela'chah* and work. Unlike Peli, who spends a great deal of time defining *mela'chah* as a way of making it understood in reference to the known "work," I claim that it is precisely the prohibition of work that is a stumbling block for American Jews. One might take me to task here and point out that there *are* many American Jews who work only five days a week and for whom it is *mela'chah* that is problematic. It is important, however, to remember the function of this rhetorical device in my work. The process of reversing expectations serves as a non-discursive argument in inviting readers into the experience of Shabbat. In writing about poetic fact I use poetic argument.

Because I richly describe the religious experience, I am able to effectively and affectively demonstrate what Mary Douglas and Suzanne Langer meant when they stated that ritual frames and controls experience. When I say that the silence before breaking bread "focuses one's attention upon the experience of initiating a meal" (72), or that "music articulates feeling in a way that words cannot" (74), these statements in context assume the utmost clarity and precision. I take Jewish ritual as seriously as Mary Douglas takes Dinka ritual. I begin with the premise that ritual has certain human functions, and I seek to make those understandable *and* inviting.

To maintain that I write non-discursively and deeply about the

---

[20]Like Abraham Heschel I generally pay careful attention to the close of major sections in my writing, and especially to the end of my chapters. At the end of Chapter 7, for instance, I write: "The business of socializing taken care of at the *kiddush*, we gather up our children and head home--the morning smell of cholent beckoning" (146). Ending a chapter with a gerund is destabilizing--there is little finality to it. I "beckon" the reader into the Shabbat as the smell of the cholent beckons me home. The reader is called to respond. Ending with the smell also nicely rounds out this chapter, which opened with a description of cholent.

Shabbat experience, however, does not answer the question: whose experience? Can I expect the reader to believe that my account of Shabbat is my complete experience of this day? Whereas Greenberg covered up for the tradition's sexism, and Peli covered up for Israeli Jews, it seems that I cover for my own self--a self that undergoes periods of religious apathy and rejection. How do I live with the tradition even when I am not buoyed by it? If every single Shabbat cannot possibly be as fulfilling as I describe it, what sustains me through the Sabbaths that are not particularly powerful? These questions go beyond the scope of this book. In fact, at several moments in my work I consciously downplay Jewish theological doctrine: twice I negate the doctrine of chosenness by emphasizing the melody of the particular prayer in which chosenness is mentioned (70-71, 144-145), and I undercut the whole prayer service in general by greatly emphasizing the sociological importance of worship (135-136). In creating apologetic theology my first instinct is not to focus in on those times when the tradition fails to be affective (and here I am in the company of Heschel, Peli, and Greenberg), or upon theological doctrines that prove divisive. Yet the reader has every right to await a future work where I will pay closer attention to the construction of my theology and to such theological issues as the interplay between thought and deed.

My writing suggests that **religion as anthropological necessity** and **religion as artful experience** can be mutually invigorating. Religion fulfills certain anthropological needs, but unless the religious life is *presented* affectively human beings will go elsewhere to satisfy those needs. **Religion as artful experience** benefits from the plausibility structure of **religion as anthropological necessity**--which argues, in part, that human beings have a *need* for artful expression. I make it clear, however, that **religion as artful experience** can more easily stand on its own in American society. Artful experience is a value that the majority culture promotes in America, whereas

religion as anthropological necessity is more problematic as persuasive strategy. I realize that American Jews, by virtue of the fact that they are human beings, are *already* engaged in activities that meet certain of their anthropological needs. If one talks of an alternative set of activities, one must realize that this calls for people to stop what they are doing currently and undertake new ways of doing things. The persuasive force of **religion as anthropological necessity**, therefore, rests upon the way it can be made alluring. *For me, **religion as anthropological necessity** and **the religious life as artful experience** meet in the rich depiction of the religious life.* Only in this deep, affectional depiction do these strategies become *persuasive*. I am not only interested in articulating strategies for sustaining religious commitment, I am interested in provoking that commitment. I seek, in other words, to influence my readers' affective *predisposition* towards religious commitment. An affective predisposition is most readily influenced by affectional writing, by non-discursive writing. The more artistically masterful this writing is, the more affective it will be. The more closely it describes the phenomenon of a particular way of life, the more that life will be intelligible. By writing a text that is affectionally alluring it is possible to affirm the art of the religious life.

CHAPTER 10

DEPICTION: *MINCHAH, SHALESHEEDIS, HAVDALAH*

Toward the latter part of Shabbat afternoon the community wakes. Children go off to "Shabbes groups,"[1] and there is much walking and visiting. As the sun begins to set, the time for *Minchah*, the afternoon service, is at hand. Two things serve to distinguish the Shabbat *Minchah* from weekday afternoon services: the first is that this is the only regular afternoon service where a portion of Torah is read;[2] the second is the special melodic interplay between *chazzan* and congregation during the repetition of the *Minchah Amidah*.

The melody of the repetition itself is not particularly beautiful; what is splendid are the periodic moments where the congregation joins in with the *chazzan* to sing groups of highlighted word-pairs. Here, for example, are the opening lines of the middle portion of the *Amidah*:

> You are One and Your Name is One; and who is like Your people Israel, one nation on earth. The splendor of greatness and the crown of salvation, the day of contentment and holiness have You given to Your people. Abraham would rejoice, Isaac would exult, Jacob and his children would rest on it, a rest of love and magnanimity, a rest of truth and faith, a rest of peace and serenity and tranquility and security, a perfect rest in which You find favor. (*Siddur* 517-519)

These lines are chanted by the *chazzan* in a sing-song fashion except that when he or she comes to "the splendor of greatness" (*"tiferet gedulah"*) and

---

[1] These are small gatherings of different children's age groups usually led by teenagers where there are stories told, traditions rehearsed, games played, and refreshments served.

[2] It is taken from the beginning of the following Shabbat's Torah portion; thus, through Scripture, the congregation begins to focus on the Shabbat and the week ahead.

"Abraham would rejoice" ("*Avraham yagail*"), the tempo breaks sharply and the whole congregation joins in. Each of these moments is composed of two words in the Hebrew. The first word acts as a sort of introduction to the second; it slowly rises in pitch, lulling the singer into a calm reverie, but then the second word dramatically plunges down the tonal scale. It is almost as if with the first word one approaches a cliff and with the second one jumps off--only to be picked up again by the continuation of the passage. No *siddur* is marked with appropriate cantillation marks delineating which words are to be so emphasized. While many congregations will accentuate the same words, it is possible for a *chazzan* to improvise, stressing different sets of words. Thus, one has to learn where to join in with the congregation. This is a playful, liturgical game, with highs and lows, peaks and valleys.

Besides the pure pleasure of singing these frolicsome words, musically these moments are important because they are wonderfully ambiguous--corresponding to the different emotions one may be feeling at this time. One person may be in particularly high spirits after a satisfying Shabbat evening, morning and afternoon; another might already be feeling the impending conclusion of Shabbat and the attendant anxieties of the work week. The melody here allows for both expressions. For the former individual, the playfulness is sheer fun--a roller coaster ride of liturgical song. For the latter, those deep, deep descending notes are times for reflection and brooding: another Shabbat come and almost gone, another week over forever.

One is supposed to have three meals on the Sabbath,[3] and the interlude between the afternoon and evening service is the designated time

---

[3]The concept of three Shabbat meals is taken from Ex. 16.25 where Moses says, in instructing the Israelites about what to do with the leftover manna portion (a double portion descended on Fridays so that no gathering needed to take place on the Sabbath): "Eat it today, for today is a Sabbath of the Lord; you will not find it today on the plain." From the three references to "today" the rabbis deduced the three mandatory meals of Shabbat (see Peli 98).

for the third meal, the *se'udah sh'lishit* in Hebrew, *shalesheedis* in Yiddish.[4] Depending upon the time of year this meal can be a full one (when Shabbat ends late and one has regained an appetite), or a small, symbolic one. The fare in most synagogues is usually limited to the pareve leftovers from the morning *kiddush*: besides some challah rolls there is gefilte fish, herring, cake, kichel. If there is a sponsor for this meal, tuna fish, eggs, chips, and salads may be added. There is much chatter, but it is subdued. One has already talked over the previous week's events, yet one is reluctant to speak about the upcoming week, for this would take away from the wholeness of the day and seem to accelerate the departure of Shabbat. (Indeed, traditionally on Shabbat one is discouraged from speaking about all activity that involves *mela'chah*--this is not considered to be *Shabbesdik* conversation.) Perhaps someone will rise and give a *d'var Torah*, a word of Torah, to further sanctify this final Shabbat meal. As the meal progresses all feel a keen sense of loss for the departing Shabbat. The mood of the congregation turns wistful, nostalgic for the Shabbat that was, longing for that "perfect rest" that does not and will not end. This is what the close of Shabbat is all about: hanging on as long as possible to the Shabbat that recedes, breathing deeply from it to sustain oneself through *chol*. We cannot make our *chol* Shabbat, though we can "Remember the Sabbath" (Ex. 20.8) all through the week.

Finally, at the end of *shalesheedis,* just before the grace after meals, the emotions felt at the departure of Shabbat are expressed in song. The most famous of these, and the most popular, is *"Mizmor le-David"* ("A Psalm of David," the twenty-third psalm).[5] Rarely does a song so perfectly capture

---

[4]The Yiddish derives from the Hebrew phrase *shalosh se'udot* (three meals). The phrase emphasizes that there are *three* significant meals on the Sabbath--as opposed to the normal two.

[5]Pinchas Peli, based upon the work of Rabbi Zvi Elimelech (an early nineteenth-century chassidic leader), speaks about the function of this psalm at *shalesheedis*: "The twilight of Sabbath afternoon is considered in the Midrash to be an hour of sadness, since Moses, the 'trustworthy shepherd,' passed away on Sabbath at that time of the day. We therefore read

one's emotions as the words and melody of this psalm. The music is haunting, poignant. The first part has a pleading quality, more beseeching God than affirming that "The Lord is my shepherd; I lack nothing. He makes me lie down in green pastures; He leads me to water in places of repose; He renews my life; He guides me in right paths as befits His name" (v. 1-3). One is struck in this opening by the mournful quality of the music, as if the singers realize that their hopes bear little chance of fruition. This feeling begins to change as the second stanza opens with "*Gam ki elech*" ("though I walk," v. 4). As opposed to the words of the first stanza that were sung unconnectedly (the loneliness of the singers being expressed musically), "*gam*" is sung more confidently and resonates comfortably onward in legato fashion--the "em" syllable is allowed to flow fully and freely till the next word. This new-found strength is needed here as we approach the darkest words of the psalm. Appropriately the melody descends as we sing: "Though I walk through a valley of deepest darkness" (v. 4). We rise remarkably quickly from this musical and literal valley to proceed with: "*lo ira' ra' ki atah imadi*" ("I fear no evil, for you are with me," v. 4). The alliteration of the two words "*ira'*" and *ra'* is brilliant, for evil becomes a poetic construct. It is suggested in song that evil (*ra'*) can be thought of as just fear (*ira'*) minus one syllable. In other words, evil only becomes evil when it is feared--but when God is "with me" evil need not be feared. Not that we may forever avoid misfortune--but that it will have no hold over us as *Malum*, for we believe in God the *Bonum*. We are impassioned now, overwhelmed with trust and confidence and we powerfully sing: "*Shivtecha u-mishantecha heimah yenachamuni*" ("Your rod and Your staff--they comfort me," v. 4). This line is sung out with such brilliance and majesty that it lifts the entire next verse

---

the Twenty-third Psalm in order to comfort ourselves in declaring that although the faithful shepherd and great teacher left us, God is still our shepherd and we shall not want" (*Shabbat Shalom* 161).

out of the psalm's melodic range by several notes: "You spread a table for me in full view of my enemies; You anoint my head with oil; my drink is abundant" (v. 5). We return to the final verse comforted but quiet once more. The tune seems poignant again but it is no longer mournful. Here is a soft affirmation and prayer that "may only goodness and steadfast love pursue me all the days of my life, and I shall dwell in the House of the Lord for many long years" (v. 6). The psalm runs out of words in this final third part and we are left to complete the song without words: "day da da dy dy dy . . ." We linger over the rising and falling syllables, playfully rehearsing the soulful passage recounted in the song.

If there is time, other songs will be sung at *shalesheedis*, expressing the approximate feelings that gave rise to the *"Mizmor le-David"*. In fact, for some people and for some synagogues there is always time because they prolong the Shabbat well past darkness. They want to hold on to Shabbat (while Shabbat must be brought in at a certain time there is more leeway in extending it). This is a perfect time for a tale of the chassidim or another kind of Jewish folk tale. A story of a pious chassidic *rebbe* is especially apposite here because characteristically it will depict the *rebbe* as a person who is able to rise to spiritual heights even in the mundane--a person who is able to sanctify his business dealings, his community responsibilities, and his personal affairs with as much *kavanah* ("intention") as he devotes to the sanctification of Shabbes. The chassidim also emphasize the *motz'ey Shabbat* (Sabbath conclusion) party called the *melavah malkah* (escorting the queen). Just as one goes to greet Shabbat late Friday afternoon, on Saturday night one accompanies the Shabbat as it takes its first steps back to its heavenly dominion.

By the time the grace after *shalesheedis* is said it is often dark. Yet significantly, the special Shabbat prayers in the grace are still recited. Shabbat does not end with darkness--it ends with *Havdalah*.

Havdalah

One would think that the rite of Havdalah ("separation") would be wide-spread amongst American Jewry. This ritual has several of the elements that have broad-range appeal for American Jews: it requires a small amount of time, it has a referent in a corresponding Christian holy day (Sunday), and it is fascinating to children. American Jews have thus warmly embraced the rituals of lighting Chanukah candles and conducting Passover Seders. Why hasn't Havdalah caught on with American Jewry? Which of the three factors has proven to be wanting in this ritual? At first one might think that it is the religious referent: in popular American culture observing Sunday means going to church on Sunday morning--there is no notion of any kind of Havdalah service. Yet this factor alone would not be decisive, for lighting Chanukah candles is not the same kind of celebration as having a Christmas mass or tree, and the Passover Seder no longer has a major referent in the celebration of Easter. The importance of the Christian religious referent is that there be a Christian holiday in the general time-frame of the Jewish holiday (and here one could even argue that Havdalah has the advantage over Chanukah candles and Passover Seders, since Shabbat unfailingly comes a day before Sunday whereas Chanukah and Christmas, and Passover and Easter are often separated by a good many days). Havdalah is also, as will become evident, quite satisfactory in piquing the interests of children.

What *has* proved Havdalah's undoing is the time element. Though Havdalah does not take more time than Chanukah candles or Passover Seders (as opposed to the Passover Seder which takes a few hours, the Havdalah may be recited in a few minutes), *it takes more commitment.* Havdalah is performed every single Saturday night fifty-two weeks of the year (plus there is a Havdalah for the conclusion of all festivals). Americans like manageable projects: we see a problem, plan for a solution, implement the plan, and then the problem goes away. Chanukah lighting and Passover

Seders are annual events. Havdalah requires a year-long commitment. Whereas lighting the Chanukah candles can be thought of as sort of a project, taking eight days and lighting different numbers of candles on each of them, Havdalah as recurring ritual smacks of the routine--one can never lay it aside for more than a week. Of course, there is no reason why a person could not recite the Havdalah every few weeks or so, or whenever he or she feels like doing it come Saturday night. But when this is a person's disposition the Havdalah usually goes unrecited for long periods of time. Though the Havdalah is a moving, poignant, beautiful ceremony it is neglected by American Jews.

Why should this be the case? Why, if a rite is left up to whenever a person feels like it, does a person rarely feel like it? Here we come to the meaning of Havdalah: Havdalah is a ritual expression of one's experience of Shabbat. The power of Havdalah grows out of the majesty of Shabbat. The more one celebrates Shabbat the more one "feels" the need for a Havdalah. *Shabbat is the affectional predisposition for Havdalah.* By and large American Jews are not *shomrei Shabbat*; by and large American Jews do not recite Havdalah. To be sure, the power, the magnificence of a ritual can serve to encourage one to pursue it again. Yet to divorce a ritual from that which affectionally predisposes commitment to that ritual is to leave performance not to feeling but to one's cultural milieu. Havdalah as just sensuous, sensory experience loses out to the numerous activities of a Saturday night that are culturally reenforced in America: going out to dinner, going to the movies, going to the theater. Havdalah only appears attractive, Havdalah is only experienced as sacred ritual, when it is perceived to be the only fitting way to conclude a Shabbat, when it is felt that there is no other proper way of getting from *kodesh* to *chol*.

All this is not to say that if one does not commit to all of the observances of Shabbat (rituals as well as prohibitions) then it is impossible to experience Shabbat on any level. This is a charge levelled at the Orthodox, occasionally with some justification, but here it is not to the point. I am trying to explain the existing state of affairs. I am trying to explain why American Jews, after an enjoyable Saturday afternoon and before a night-on-the-town, do not perform the Havdalah service. If one separates the ritual from its larger framework, in this case Havdalah from Shabbat, then commitment to that ritual is deprived of its plausibility structure. Commitment to Havdalah without commitment to Shabbat becomes commitment to lighting a candle, smelling some spices, drinking some wine, singing some songs: all very nice activities but hardly worth committing to every Saturday night--unless one feels the need for Havdalah, unless one cannot begin Saturday night without it, unless one cannot surrender Shabbat without its blessings.

At the close of Shabbat there is a melancholy gladness in the air. One is thankful for the Shabbat that was, yet one feels the loss of the departing *neshamah yeterah* (extra soul).[6] It is interesting to note that the Shabbat is already over before the actual ceremony of Havdalah begins. That is, though one is not supposed to eat before Havdalah, the prohibition on *mela'chah* ends with the weekday evening *Amidah* on Saturday night which includes a special "havdalah" paragraph.[7] We do not need the ceremony of Havdalah

---

[6]In the Talmud, Rabbi Simeon ben Lakish remarks that "an extra soul does the Holy One, blessed-be-He, install into man on the eve on the Sabbath. As the Sabbath goes out--the extra soul departs" (*Talmud Bavli, Betza* 16a; qtd. in Peli 92). Peli adds: "We may say that it [the extra soul] is the holy spirit which is within us, and which comes to the fore on the Sabbath. It is also according to the same source [Rabbi Nachman in *Zohar Chadash*] the invisible crown that human beings all wear, similar to the crown worn by the ministering angels. The Sabbath comes to remind us of this holy spirit, this extra dimension of our soul, which is within us, and which we keep imprisoned for six days of toil. It comes to open our eyes to see the holy crown above us which we barred our eyes from seeing during the six days" (92).

[7]The "havdalah" paragraph is inserted into the fourth blessing of the *Amidah* after the words "You graciously endow man with wisdom and teach insight to a frail mortal." It conveys the essential idea that God has "distinguished between the sacred and the secular, between light and darkness, between Israel and the peoples, between the seventh day and

to allow us to do work, we need Havdalah to express our love and longing for Shabbat.

Havdalah is recited both in the synagogue and in the home. It is a more special experience at home, or in a small group, because physically one is able to feel more. The electric lights in the house are turned down, the multi-wicked Havdalah candle is lit, the leader raises the cup of wine and we sing: "Behold! God is my salvation, I shall trust and not fear--for God is my might and my praise--the Lord was a salvation for me. You can draw water with joy, from the springs of salvation [Isaiah 12.2-3]." The melody is spritely, sung with enthusiasm. After these first words there is a chance to break off and just mouth some syllables without words--we go beyond words. As we sing we look about us at the faces aglow with the candle light. The flickering shadows hauntingly urge us to appreciate each other here and now: in the grand scheme of things our presence on Earth is but like these flames--we flit in, we flit out. In some families the Havdalah is recited with everyone arm in arm or holding hands; we joy in each other's touch, take comfort in each other's physical support. My children Nathan and Rebecca go absolutely ga-ga over the candle. The flickering light, accented by the dark room, is particularly mesmerizing to them.

Salvation, *yeshu'ah*, is the key word of the Havdalah. There were three references to "salvation" in the opening lines, and the word will appear several times more in the service. It is quite appropriate to emphasize salvation at this point, for there is both anxiety and hope associated with it-- emotions intimately connected with what one feels at the close of Shabbat. One hopes for salvation, one affirms that "God is my salvation," but in the

---

the six days of labor" (*Siddur* 269). Unless indicated otherwise, "Havdalah" is to be taken for the whole ceremony normally performed shortly after the *Amidah* on Saturday night. It should also be mentioned here that technically once it is dark a person need not even pray the *Amidah* in order to do *mela'chah*: a simple "Blessed are You who separates holy from profane" will suffice.

absence of the Messiah it is clear that the world has most definitely not been saved, that humanity has not experienced salvation. Similarly, at the conclusion of Shabbat, one is suffused with the divine presence--yet the *neshamah yeterah* departs leaving one in discomfort (alleviated in part by the smelling of spices), and staring anxiously at the long hard week ahead.

The opening few lines of the Havdalah were sung bravely and confidently. Afterwards the leader proceeds alone, chanting the next few lines: "Salvation is the Lord's, Your blessing be upon Your people! *Selah*" (Psalm 46.12).[8] Then, we arrive at the climactic moment of the service as the leader cries out: "God, save! May the King answer us on the day we call" (Psalm 20.10). In response to this call all chant the next line (taken from the book of Esther) with great fervor: "For the Jews there was light, gladness, joy, and honor--so may it be for us" (Esther 8.16). Significantly, we invoke a time when Jews were in need and when God came to the rescue. We have reason to affirm that God is indeed our salvation.

The mood of the Havdalah shifts as the section of the blessings is recited: first over wine, then over spices, then over fire.[9] The blessings are said somberly, focusing one's attention upon the attendant ritual action. After the recitation of the blessing over the wine the cup is put down--the wine will be drunk at the end of the whole ceremony. Next comes the

---

[8]This line is immediately followed by two other verses from the Psalms: "God, Master of legions, praised is the man who trusts in You" (Psalm 84.13); "The Lord of hosts is with us; the God of Jacob is our haven. *Selah*" (Psalm 46.12).

[9]Pinchas Peli says here: "This order was seen by Jewish mystics as representing a succession in the refinement of our senses, from the lower to the higher: the wine must be taken *into* one's mouth and tasted before one can enjoy it; the fragrance of the *besamim* (spices) could be sensed even when held *near* one's nostrils; the sight of the burning candle could be sensed even from *afar*, and the highest sense of all, the conceptual discerning taking place in the mind, could be applied to the abstract and utterly ephemeral. This elevating succession is reflected in the structure of the human face going upward from the mouth (tasting), to the nose (smelling), to the eyes (seeing), and eventually to the mind, which discerns spiritually and intellectually between good and bad, the holy and the profane, the rest of the week and the Sabbath (*Shabbat Shalom* 116).

blessing over the spices: "Blessed are You, Lord our God, King of the universe, *borei minay besamim*, who creates species of fragrance." There are different customs for the types of spices to be used; the most popular are cinnamon and cloves. The *besamim* are stored in a special, ornately decorated spice box--some made of wood, others made of silver. Traditional *besamim* boxes remind one of palatial towers, and contain a small door which when opened reveals a treasure trove of fragrant cloves and cinnamon sticks. Some Sephardic Jews use liquid *besamim* made out of extracts of spices. This custom works wonderfully well in large groups such as at synagogue. The *besamim* are squirted onto the hands of each congregant as the opening paragraph is chanted, and at the time of its blessing all lift their hands to their noses for a collective "Ahhh." (Though only the few people immediately surrounding the leader get a chance to smell the *besamim* in Ashkenazic synagogues, the congregation playfully sighs "Ahhh" at the appropriate moment.) At home, since the group is small, we wait until everyone has a chance to smell from the *besamim*. It has been wonderful seeing the transformation in my son through the various Havdalahs of his life. At first as a very small infant when we passed the *besamim* box under his nose he did not react much; then when he got a bit older he instinctively would open his mouth as we moved this thing in front of his face; now, he ever so cutely breathes through his nose at the *besamim* (whether he smells it or not is another story). If I am leading the Havdalah I like to smell the *besamim* again after it has made the rounds. I seem to need the comfort that the spices provide in order to enter the most solemn of the blessings: "Blessed are you, Lord our God, King of the universe, *borei me'oray ha-aish*, who creates the illuminations of the fire." As we recite this blessing we press our cupped hands against the light of the fire, visually reflecting upon the light and dark cast by the shadows of our fingers upon the palms of our hands. We are struck with awe gazing at the fire. At this moment we know that indeed God is *borei me'oray ha-aish*," that only God could have created fire, that humankind borrowed from God when it kindled the first flame. There is an eerie quality to holding this torch aloft inside our home. The flames seem to be struggling to ascend to the heavens, imitating the departing *neshamah yeterah*. The potential for good and the potential for evil are manifest in the flames. Fire can provide warmth, fire can destroy. God created fire: we put it to use.

The Havdalah concludes with a blessing that praises God who "separates between holy and secular, between light and darkness, between Israel and the nations, between the seventh day and the six days of labor. Blessed are you, Lord, *ha-mavdil bein kodesh le-chol*, who separates between holy and secular" (*Siddur* 621). Here at the end of Shabbat is a serious declaration of chosenness. This declaration serves to uplift our now lonely souls--our *neshamah yeterah* might have abandoned us but God never will.

The Havdalah is over. In some families, a small portion of wine is poured out into a dish and the candle is extinguished; in my own we usually blow out the candle and, as the final spark or two of the dying embers on the wick evaporate, we sing the chillingly beautiful "*Eliyahu Ha-Navi*": "Elijah the prophet, Elijah the Tishbi, Elijah the Giladi. He will come to us in our days, with the Messiah--son of David." This is a comforting song, sung with quiet determination and affirmation; but it is also a plea: though the Messiah has not arrived we await him nevertheless. At this moment all our dead seem eerily near. As our extra souls disengage themselves from our bodies they mingle with souls whose bodies are no longer. We feel the presence of all these souls and remember their lives here on earth--how they lived, how they loved. The millions of victims in the Holocaust also come to mind and heart here--how they were murderously stopped from living and from loving. We recall the companion song to "*Eliyahu Ha-Navi*," the "*Ani Ma'amin*" ("I believe") with its line: "*Im kol zeh achakeh lo be-chol yom she-yavo*, even with all of this [tarrying], every day I will await his [the Messiah's] arrival." In spite of being ushered out from the presence of the sweet Sabbath, we go on with our lives. Yet the Shabbat has left its mark on us. Indeed, some have the custom of lightly dipping their fingers into the Havdalah wine, and then touching their eyelids and the insides of their pockets with them. This physically affirms what we all know we now bring with us into the work-week: a taste of Shabbat.

CONCLUSION

The world is contingent on creation, and the worth of history depends on redemption. To be a Jew is to affirm the world without being enslaved to it; to be a part of civilization and to go beyond it; to conquer space and to sanctify time. Judaism is *the art of surpassing civilization*, sanctification of time, sanctification of history.

Abraham Heschel[1]

One might venture to regard the obsessional neurosis as a pathological counterpart to the formation of a religion, to describe this neurosis as a private religious system, and religion as a universal obsessional neurosis. The essential resemblance would lie in the fundamental renunciation of the satisfaction of inherent instincts, and the chief difference in the nature of these instincts, which in the neurosis are exclusively sexual, but in religion are of egoistic origin.

Sigmund Freud[2]

In presenting the religious life in an anthropocentric framework, one must at last confront the problem of reductionism. Unless one is prepared to take seriously Heschel's claim that "Judaism is the art of surpassing civilization," one risks a ride on the slippery slope towards Freud's "religion as a universal obsessional neurosis." Heschel's phrase stands in sharp contrast to Mordecai Kaplan's *magnum opus, Judaism as a Civilization.* Indeed Heschel, in placing added emphasis on his remark about *surpassing* civilization, seems pointedly to take on Kaplan's work.

Heschel cautions that "human existence cannot derive its ultimate

---

[1] *God In Search of Man: A Philosophy of Judaism* 418.
[2] Sigmund Freud, "Obsessive Acts and Religious Practices," 1907, Trans. R. C. McWatters, *Character and Culture* (New York: Macmillan, 1963) 25.

206

meaning from society, because society itself is in need of meaning. It is as legitimate to ask: Is mankind needed?--as it is to ask: Am I needed?" (MNA 196). Heschel could thus argue that **religion as anthropological necessity** merely postpones the existential question of need: viewing the religious life as intelligible in that it satisfies basic human needs gives one no help in answering that question, "Why am I needed?" Heschel states emphatically, therefore: "Let us not confound . . . religion with the use which man makes of it. . . . As long as man sees in religion the satisfaction of his own needs, a guarantee for immortality or a device to protect society, it is not God whom he serves but himself. The more removed from the ego, the more real is His presence. It is a sure way of missing Him when we think that God is an answer to a human need, as if not only armies, factories and movies, but God, too, had to cater to the ego" (MNA 232-234). Heschel turns the tables on Freud, claiming that it is precisely when religion is "of egoistic origin" that it can be reduced to something like an obsessional neurosis. In this case however, says Heschel, one is really not talking about religion at all, but about a human construct. Heschel absolutely affirms that God exists independently of human beings, that God is not a product of the human. He adds: "Religion as an institution, the Temple as an ultimate end, or, in other words, religion for religion's sake, is idolatry. . . . Religion is for God's sake. The human side of religion, its creeds, rituals and institutions, is a way rather than the goal. The goal is 'to do justice, to love mercy and to walk humbly *with* thy God.' When the human side of religion becomes the goal, injustice becomes a way" (MNA 236-237). One could say, then, that for Heschel presenting the religious life as one of anthropological necessity, as I do here, not only misses what religion is about but borders on the idolatrous. He sees no way to move to God if one begins with the human being.

If Heschel is implicitly critical of a narrow presentation of the religious life as anthropological necessity, he also comes out strongly against viewing the religious life simply as artful experience:

> The fact is that we do not turn to art in order to gratify, but in order to foster interests and feelings. A work of art introduces us to emotions which we have never cherished before. It is boring unless we are surprised by it. Great works produce rather than satisfy needs by giving the world fresh craving. By expressing things we were not even aware of, works of art inspire new ends, unanticipated visions. . . . Morality and religion do not begin as feelings within man but as responses to goals and situations outside of man. It is always in regard to an objective situation that we judge and assert it is right or wrong; and it is in answer to what is beyond the ineffable that man says yes to God. (MNA 218-220)

Religion for Heschel does not begin with the Schleiermachian "feeling of absolute dependency"; religion begins as a response to God. For Heschel, the religious life is more *artful response* than artful experience or expression. The religious life is true not because it fosters a rich emotional life, but because God ordained it. God teaches human beings through the religious life just what feelings are worthwhile. In a way reminiscent of David Tracy, Heschel suggests that religion (like great art) is not boring, and that religion is truly exciting when the human being is surprised by God--the ultimate artist.

Religion as artful experience stands in contrast to Heschel's words here. It argues that the religious life can be conveyed and appreciated as art. From this perspective, theological accounts of the religious life are to be judged by the force of their rhetoric and by their literary allure. This strategy seems to accept the standards of a secular consumer society which dictate that religion has nothing to contribute to a person's intellectual growth, and positions religion in the most appealing market available to it: that of artful experience. Heschel, though, reminds us time and again that religion is not a way to grow intellectually or emotionally, but a way to grow close to God: "*Religion begins with God's question and man's answer*"; "Religion is for God's sake. The human side of religion, its creeds, rituals, and institutions, is a way rather than the goal" (MNA 76, 237). Heschel strove to awaken his readers to God--not to their own emotional or intellectual vitality. The value of the religious life for Heschel is that through it a dialogue forms between God and human being. If this is not the case religion will have nothing to say to a person; religion will not be able to lift a person up from a narrow egoistic existence.[3] Heschel insists that the religious life must always be presented theocentrically. Ultimately, meaning emerges not from the relation of art to viewer or from society to individual, but from human being to God. The only way to go from concern to ultimacy, from meaning to ultimate meaning, is by responding to God. The reduction of religion to artful experience, therefore, is potentially as treacherous for Heschel as the reduction of religion to anthropological necessity: both border on the idolatrous.

One returns to a phrase that Heschel prints verbatim in *God in Search of Man* and in *Man is Not Alone*: "If man is not more than human, then he is less than human. Man is but a short, critical stage between the animal and the spiritual. His state is one of constant wavering, of soaring or descending. Undeviating humanity is nonexistent. The emancipated man is yet to emerge" (MNA 211).[4] Heschel's depiction of the scale of humanness as a slope (on which one either goes up or down) has a parallel in the Jewish tradition: for every day that one does not increase one's knowledge of Torah,

---

[3]Heschel thus states: "The greatest problem is not how to continue but how to exalt our existence. The cry for a life beyond the grave is presumptuous, if there is no cry for eternal life prior to our descending to the grave. Eternity is not perpetual future but perpetual presence. He has planted in us the seed of eternal life. The world to come is not only a hereafter but also a *herenow*. Our greatest problem is not how to continue but how to return. 'How can I repay unto the Lord all his bountiful dealings with me?' (Psalm 116.12). When life is an answer, death is a home-coming" (MNA 295-296).

[4]In *God In Search of Man* Heschel writes: "What we have learned from Jewish history is that if a man is not more than human then he is less than human. Judaism is an attempt to prove that in order to be a man, you have to be more than a man, that in order to be a people we have to be more than a people. Israel was made to be a 'holy people.' This is the essence of its dignity and the essence of its merit. Judaism is a link to eternity, kinship with ultimate reality" (422).

a gulf of two days is created--one day for the Torah not learned, one for the Torah unlearned (forgotten).[5] It thus requires twice the effort to regain Torah knowledge as it does to lose it. There is no neutral ground in the learning of Torah, there is no neutral ground in the learning of what it means to be a human being. The only way to move up the scale of humanness is to respond to that which is divine. When God is the magnet guiding one's humanity, one is drawn away from the ephemeral and toward the everlasting. When religion is limited solely to the human it gradually *descends* to meet reductionist conceptions of it. Precisely then religion has nothing to teach one about how to take the risks--economic, physical, social, political--that help one to be more than human.

Heschel's words are indeed necessary cautions in avoiding reductionism in religion. The problem of reductionism, however, does not seem to be the most immediate scandal for religion. The key problem today is still that problem articulated by Mordecai Kaplan in 1920: "How to get our people sufficiently interested in religion to want a ritual." To concentrate on reductionism is to presuppose that people are interested enough in religion to want to reduce it--a presupposition unwarranted in our society. It is a question of emphasis. One does not wish to reduce religion to the point where transcendence disappears, but, if one is convinced that the religious life is worth sustaining, one also wants to interest people in ritual. Herein lies the importance of seeing **religion as anthropological necessity** and **religion as artful experience** as *heuristic approaches* in exploring the art of the religious life. These strategies keep the religious orientation viable so that Jews may continue to discover and rediscover, through ritual coherence and spiritual continuity, the authenticity of Jewish religious life that Heschel

---

[5]The phrase as recounted by Rashi in his commentary on Deut. 11.13 is *"im ta'azveni yom, yomayim e'ezveka,"* "if you leave Me for a day I will leave you for two days." See *Talmud Yerushalmi B'rachot* (Jerusalem Talmud, "Blessings" tractate) 110b for two other very similar versions.

indicates at the limits of articulable experience. By pursuing the religious life, albeit through a heuristic approach such as **religion as anthropological necessity** or **religion as artful experience**, one may ultimately come upon a moment of "eureka"--when the divine is revealed.[6] Heschel is not concerned with heuristic approaches to the religious life. As a result, one either finds oneself within the tradition about which Heschel so movingly writes, or one looks on and feels the beauty that Heschel feels for that tradition. A specific *way* into that tradition, however, is not disclosed.

Here is where the strength of Mordecai Kaplan's work comes into play. Kaplan boldly reduces Judaism to a religion without supernaturalism. He interests Jews in their religion by arguing that the Jewish religion is the cornerstone of the Jewish civilization. But why was Kaplan able to interest Jews in their civilization? Because Kaplan was correct in positing the importance of the "intense social emotions in the human being" (JAC 332). Earlier I claimed that **religion as anthropological necessity** gives rational backing to "Judaism as a civilization." It can now be seen, too, that the persuasiveness of "Judaism as a civilization" rests on the *emotional* backing of **religion as anthropological necessity**--*now used in its widest sense* to include not just the human as the social, symbol using being, but the human as the emotional being. "Judaism as a civilization" is persuasive because humans are rational *and* emotional beings. Jews, as human beings with intense social emotions, need to bond with other human beings, and "Judaism as a civilization" provides the Jews with an enormous outlet for their social emotions: every single Jewish person in the Jewish civilization regardless of religious belief or practice.

Kaplan's one major failing was that he did not articulate how the intense social emotions of the human being could be expressed and enhanced

---

[6]The word "eureka," one recalls, shares the same Greek root (*heurisko*: find) with the word "heuristic."

through ritual. As a result, he tends to reduce Jewish ritual to certain abstract meanings. When *this* reduction occurs he undercuts the performance of Jewish ritual and it can then indeed be reduced away. Through his first reduction, "Judaism without supernaturalism," Kaplan succeeds in getting people interested in religion. Through his second reduction of ritual to abstract meanings, he fails to get people "to want a ritual."

In this work I have built upon Kaplan's success and have tried to correct for his mistakes. I write in the anthropocentric framework of Judaism without supernaturalism, but I argue for and write rich depictions of ritual. I encourage readers to "want a ritual" by *showing* how the religious life is an anthropological necessity and is artful experience. In doing so I also write of moments when the religious life--even if entered into and sustained by means of anthropocentric strategies--needs to have access to the vocabulary of transcendence: of awe, holiness, wonder, mystery, and the sacred. "*Na'aseh ve-nishma'*," it is written (Ex. 24.7): "We will do and we will listen." When we are sufficiently interested and committed to "*na'aseh*," to ritual action, we will again be ready to listen to the voice of God. Indeed, we may come to realize, as did the Jews at Sinai, that God is already speaking quite eloquently through the human being's performance of ritual.

BIBLIOGRAPHY

Berger, Peter. *The Sacred Canopy: Elements of a Sociological Theory of Religion*. New York: Doubleday, 1967.

Bergson, Henri. *The Two Sources of Morality and Religion*. 1932. Trans. R. Ashley Audra and Cloudesley Brereton. New York: H. Holt and Co., 1935.

Bernstein, Richard J. *Beyond Objectivism and Relativism: Science, Hermeneutics, and Praxis*. Philadelphia: University of Pennsylvania Press, 1985.

Cassirer, Ernst. *An Essay on Man: An Introduction to a Philosophy of Human Culture*. New Haven: Yale University Press, 1944.

The Complete ArtScroll Siddur: Weekday/Sabbath/Festival, Nusach [tradition of] *Ashkenaz*. Trans. Nosson Scherman. New York: Mesorah Publications, 1984.

Douglas, Mary. *Purity and Danger: An Analysis of the Concepts of Pollution and Taboo*. London: ARK, 1966.

Durkheim, Emile. *The Elementary Forms of the Religious Life*. Trans. Joseph Ward Swain. 1915. New York: Free Press, 1965.

Eliade, Mircea. *The Quest: History and Meaning in Religion*. Chicago: The University of Chicago Press, 1969.

Farley, Margaret. *A Study in the Ethics of Commitment within the Context of Theories of Human Love and Temporality*. Diss. Yale University, 1974.

Freud, Sigmund. "Obsessive Acts and Religious Practices." 1907. *Character and Culture*. Trans. R. C. Mcwatters. New York: Macmillan, 1963. 17-26.

Fromm, Erich. *The Art of Loving*. 1956. New York: Harper & Row, 1974.

Greenberg, Irving. *The Jewish Way: Living the Holidays*. New York: Summit, 1988.

Guardini, Romano. *The Spirit of the Liturgy*. Trans. Ada Lane. London: Sheed & Ward, 1937.

The Haggadah. Trans. Joseph Elias. New York: Mesorah Publications, 1977.

Heschel, Abraham Joshua. *God in Search of Man: A Philosophy of Judaism*. Philadelphia: Jewish Publication Society, 1955.

---. *Man is Not Alone: A Philosophy of Religion*. 1951. New York: Farrar, Straus & Giroux, 1988.

---. *The Sabbath: Its Meaning for Modern Man*. New York: Farrar, Straus and Young, 1951.

Huizinga, Johan. *Homo Ludens: A Study of the Play-Element in Culture*. 1944. New York: Roy Publishers, 1950.

James, William. *The Varieties of Religious Experience: A Study in Human Nature*. 1902. New York: NAL Penguin, 1958.

Kaplan, Mordecai M. *Judaism as a Civilization: Toward a Reconstruction of American Jewish Life*. 1934. Philadelphia: Jewish Publication Society, 1981.

---. *Judaism Without Supernaturalism: The only alternative to Orthodoxy and Secularism*. New York: Reconstructionist Press, 1967.

---. *The Meaning of God in Modern Jewish Religion*. 1937. New York: Reconstructionist Press, 1962.

---. "A Program for the Reconstruction of Judaism." *The Menorah Journal* 6 (August 4, 1920) 181-193. Rpt. as "The Reconstruction of Judaism." *The Jew in the Modern World: A Documentary History*. Ed. Paul R. Mendes-Flohr and Jehuda Reinharz. New York: Oxford University Press, 1980. 396-399.

Langer, Susanne K. *Feeling and Form: A Theory of Art Developed from Philosophy in a New Key*. New York: Charles Scribner's Sons, 1953.

---. *Philosophy in a New Key: A Study in the Symbolism of Reason, Rite, and Art*. New York: Mentor, 1948.

Lash, Nicholas. *Voices of Authority*. Shepherdstown: Patmos, 1976.

MacIntyre, Alasdair. *After Virtue: A Study in Moral Theory*. Notre Dame: University of Notre Dame Press, 1984.

Otto, Rudolf. Introduction. *On Religion: Speeches to its Cultured Despisers*. By Friedrich Schleiermacher. 1799. Trans. John Oman. New York: Harper & Row, 1958. vii-xx.

Peli, Pinchas H. *Shabbat Shalom: A Renewed Encounter With the Sabbath*. Washington, D.C.: B'nai Brith Books, 1988.

Schleiermacher, Friedrich. *On Religion: Speeches to its Cultured Despisers*. 1799. Trans. John Oman. New York: Harper & Row, 1958.

Toulmin, Stephen. *The Uses of Argument*. Cambridge: University Press, 1958.

Tracy, David. *Plurality and Ambiguity: Hermeneutics, Religion, Hope*. San Francisco: Harper & Row, 1987.

Unamuno, Miguel de. *The Tragic Sense of Life in Men and in Peoples*. Trans. J. E. Crawford Flitch. 1921. London: Macmillan and Co., 1926.

INDEX OF NAMES

STUDIES IN RELIGION AND SOCIETY